SAN MIGUEL ISLAND

Santa Barbara's Fourth Island West

by Lois J. Roberts

SAN MIGUEL ISLAND
Santa Barbara's Fourth Island West

is published by

Cal Rim Books
24694 Upper Trail
Carmel, California 93923

ISBN 0-9630370-0-5
Designed by Marilyn McCracken

Cataloging Data
Roberts, Lois J.
SAN MIGUEL ISLAND, Santa Barbara's Fourth Island West

Bibliography: p.
Includes index
1. San Miguel Island (California)—History. 2. Channel Island Indians. 3. Natural History. 4. Industry—Sea mammal oil and sheep. 5. Marine ecology—diving—National Park.
I. Title
Library of Congress Catalog Card Number 91-73715
ISBN 0-9630370-5-0

CONTENTS

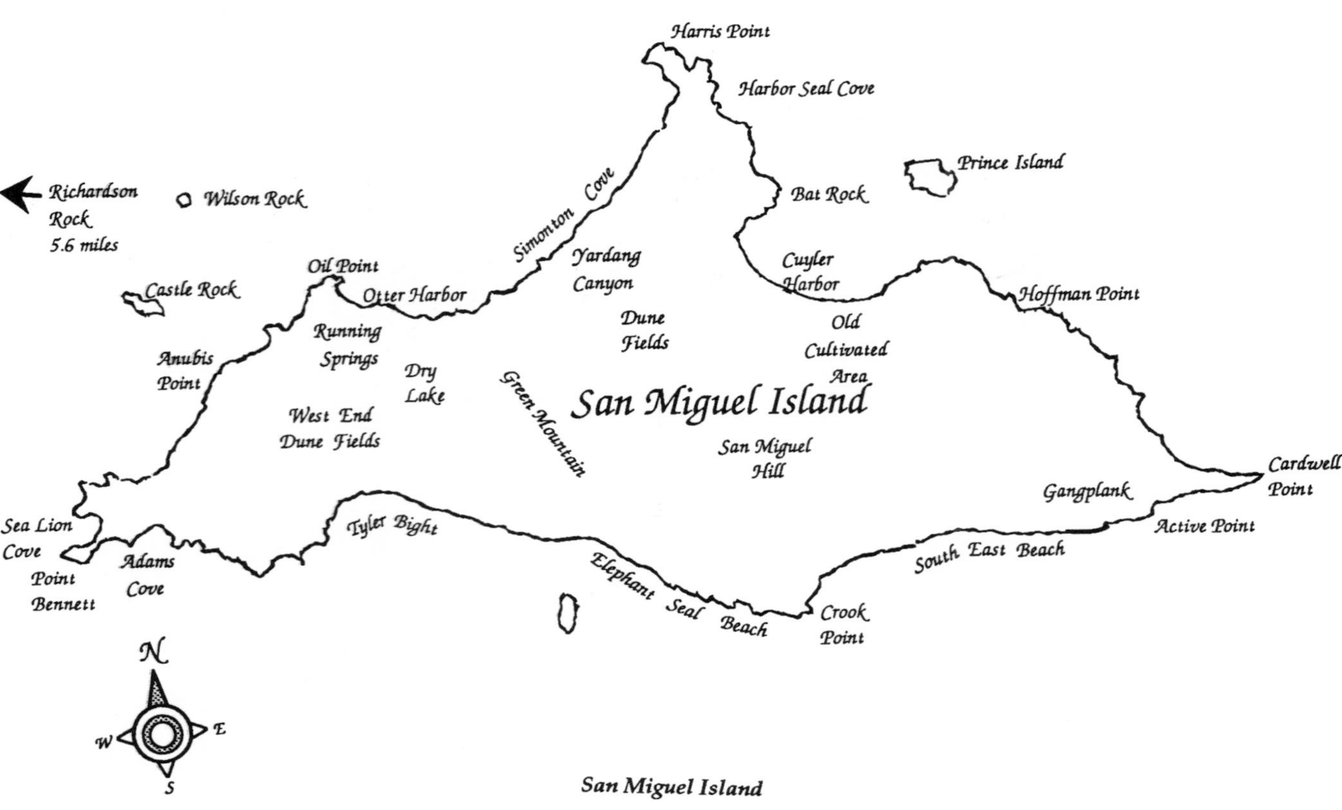

San Miguel Island

Foreword

This book is for lovers of the Santa Barbara Channel Islands, but importantly too, it is for students who would enjoy a short microcosm of California history. Surprisingly, this island experienced many of the frontier events common to other parts of California and even modern events such as World War II. Dramatic ecological episodes took place on San Miguel Island during the last century and a half. Following upon thousands of years of human habitation, the island's ancient pristine nature and its isolation in a rich marine environment suffered the negative impact of exotic western man. San Miguel Island had been a sort of Galapagos Island before it was caught up in the web of our mainland and national history. The present regeneration of its soils, lush grasses, rare species, and especially the return of the once exterminated sea mammals gives us hope.

Apparently San Miguel Island has excited the soul of just about every specialist who has beheld it. Natural history museums sent out their people on a regular basis for decades. Then, thanks to Congressional budgets in the 1970's, budgets tailored to fulfill national environmental protection laws, the National Park Service contracted for studies by archaeologists, paleontologists, biologists, myself and many others. I was a newcomer to a band of dedicated island researchers, and I benefited from their years of effort when I began work on this book.

Mel Chambers, a young pioneer in the field of cultural resource management, involved me in this project in 1978, and I thank him and Phil DeBarros at the Chambers Group in Santa Ana for giving me this and other challenging assignments.

Perhaps the first non-researcher I should thank is my duaghter Susan, who at age seven back in 1979 was just tall enough to reach the controls on the Channel Islands National Monument copy machine. Out of that machine came the initial data. Susan is in college now, thus defining the very long time this book has been underway. Like the researchers I approached to help me, I taught classes and worked as a consultant. I shoved these chapters to the back of my desk; and as I sent them out for review by my fellow island watchers, they did the same. Yet, they steadily gave of their expertise and I thank them.

In those early National Park Monument days, Nick Whelan and Bill Ehorn got me started and Headquarters staff flew me out to San Miguel Island and opened up their files to me. The archivists who helped me are too numerous to mention by name. They included staff at the Huntington Library, at the Bancroft Library, at the Archaeological Clearing House and Library at the University of California Santa Barbara, at several National Archives and Records Centers, and at Coast Guard, Navy and other military facilities in Long Beach, California and in Washington, D.C. Still, it was the participants in the island's history who allowed me interviews and provided the missing links who made this a somewhat complete story. Among them were the children of the sheep ranchers, Robert Brooks and Herbert Lester.

The specialists who reviewed and gave me suggestions for chapters outside of the usual boundaries of the historian included Donald Johnson who helped me in my synthesis of his research on landscape evolution. Archaeologists Michael Glassow, John Johnson and Pandora Smethkamp guided my research on the Indian past while Chester King and Don Morris read those chapters. Pinniped specialists Dana Seagars and Robert de Long at NOAA, and Jerry Loomis and Chuck Woodhouse either read or contributed to the marine mammal chapter. Paleontologist Daniel A. Guthrie supplied his recent publications and read portions of the chapter on flora and fauna. Steve Junak supplied ideas for my flora research and Dan Gotshall and Gary Davis commented upon the chapter. Captain John Caldwell who once worked on a lighthouse tender that serviced the Richardson Rock buoy helped with navigational aids. Peter Howorth advised on shipwrecks. Writers Augusta Fink and Allan Marcus, and Island Rangers Robert Danno, Mike Maki and Allen Fieldson helped me revise the work on excursions to the island. California historians Dave Williams and Kaye Briegel read and commented upon the entire manuscript.

Marilyn McCracken, an artist by education, created the maps, edited and typeset the text, and offered her creativity to every aspect of the publication. Publishers Dan Gotshall, Ed Zolkoski, and Bill McNally answered technical questions. As always, thanks goes to the Women Writers Computer Group of Beverly Hills for their support, ideas, and enthusiasm.

Finally, however, the research is mine, and any inaccuracies and misinterpretations are faults of my own making.

Photographic Acknowledgements

William F. Bryan, a genius at capturing animal behavior, generously contributed the cover photo, and the pictures of the otters.

Thanks are due to the following for letting me select photographs out of their wonderful collections and for giving me permission to use those I was able to include. Individual credits are listed with each picture:

Robert Brooks Collection
Chambers Group
Dana Gotshall
Mike Maki
National Park Service
Betsy Lester Roberti
Bill Roberts
Dana Seagars
Mary Valentine

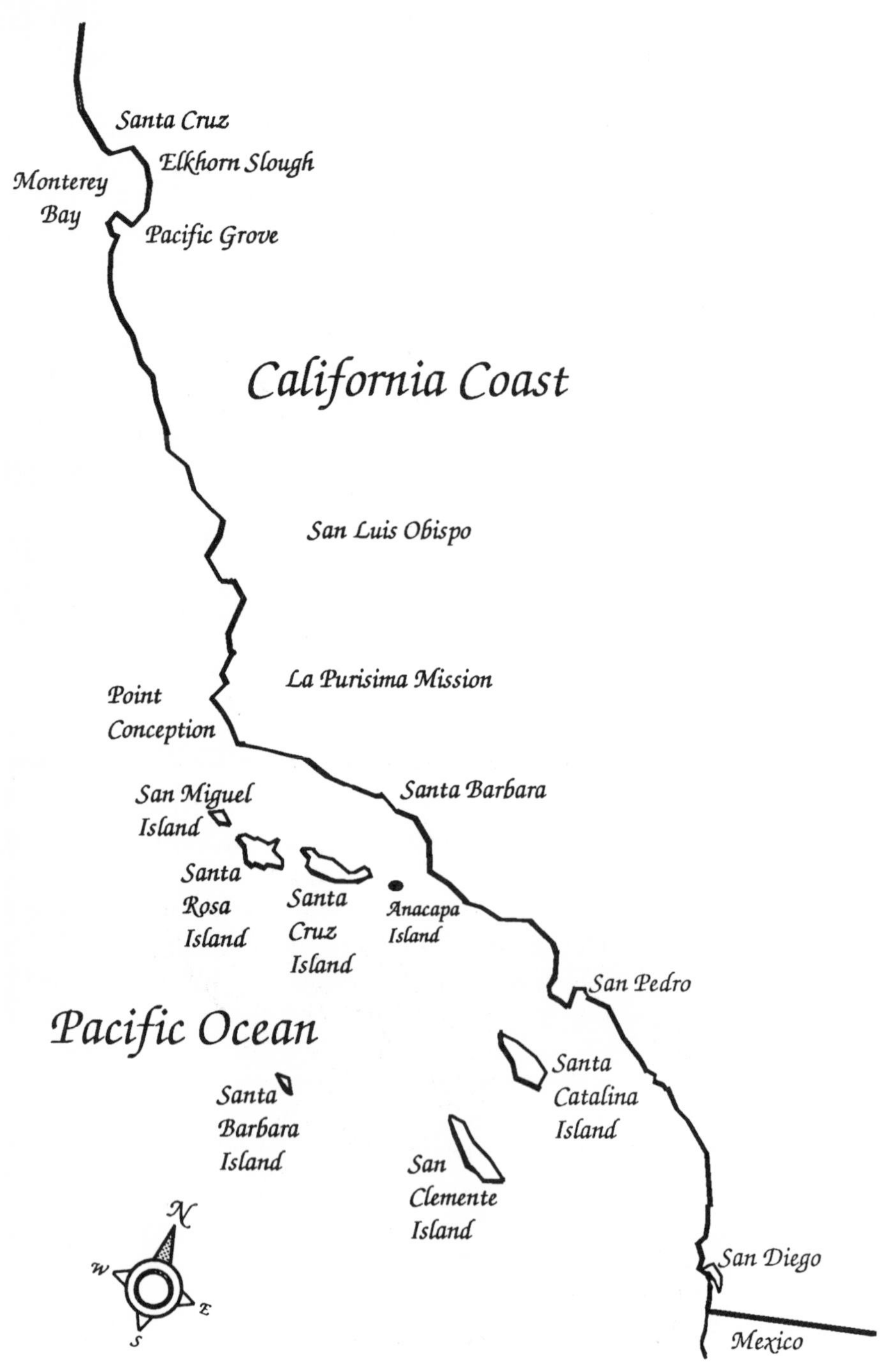

Map of the California Bight

Chapter I

INTRODUCTION
San Miguel Island: The Beginning

This is a book about a rather young island, probably uplifted in the late Pleistocene some 700,000 years ago. Its two mountain peaks first rose from the sea as islets near California's great seaward promontory, Point Conception. This is also the account of the people who managed to live or work on San Miguel's sea-shaped mesas generation after generation 10,000 years or more. Scientific data tells us that man has shared the island with pygmy elephants, fur seals, a small fox, and with many other living things.

San Miguel Island lies at the western extremity of the great Southern California Bight, a bay extending from the Mexican border to Point Conception. In all, eight islands lie off Southern California, and the most westerly of the eight are called the Northern Channel Islands. Approaching them from east to west they are Anacapa, Santa Cruz, Santa Rosa, and finally San Miguel. Evidence suggests that

Channel Islands National Park

The tiny fox, descended from early inhabitants of San Miguel.

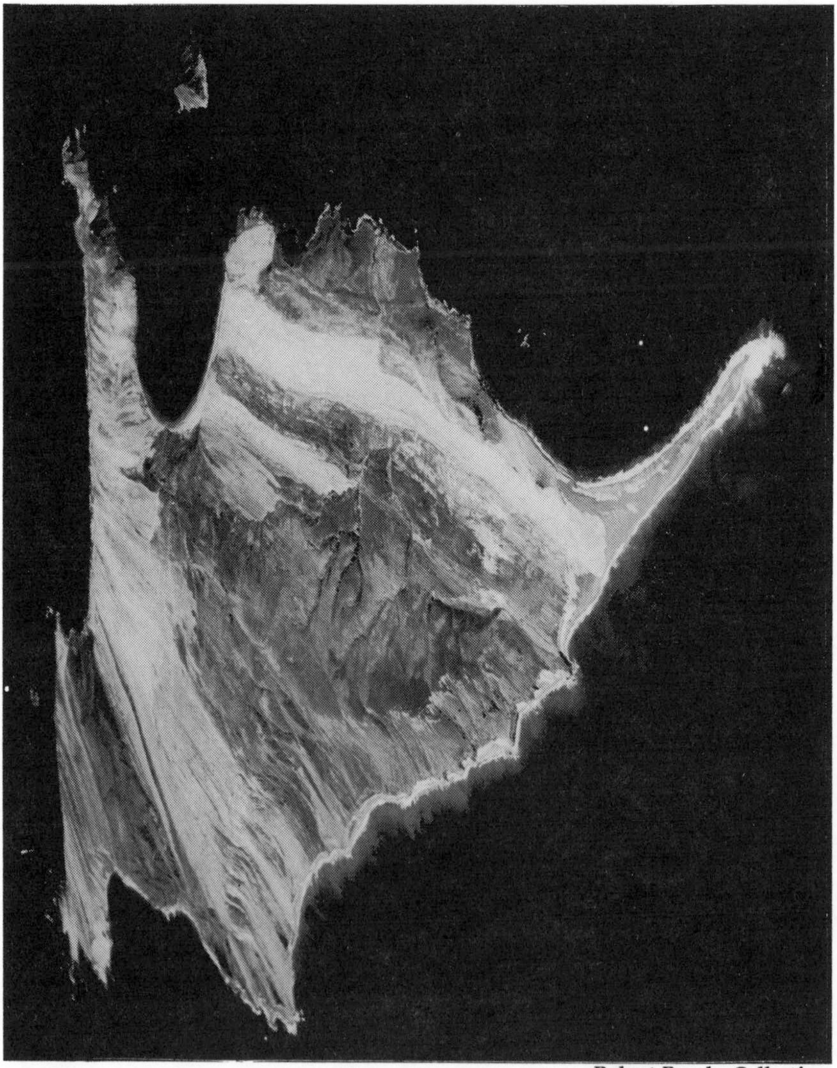

After sheep grazing stripped the island of vegetation, northwest winds swept sand from the north coast overland into Cuyler Harbor and across the entire island. 1930's.

Robert Brooks Collection

during glacial times the four comprised a single island, Santarosae.[1]

As the world sea levels rose and the lowlands were submerged Santarosae broke up into four islands which in landform still resembled the parent island: narrow, mesa-like Anacapa, large and mountainous Santa Cruz and eastern Santa Rosa, then a drop to tableland on western Santa Rosa and all of San Miguel.

Climate, Shape, and Size

A traveler driving north from Santa Barbara on the California coast highway may occasionally glimpse a view of the island as it appears as a low mound on the horizon just before turning inland at the Gaviota Pass. Yet, much of the time it is shrouded in fog and coastal stratus and never seen at all. Observers standing atop the mountains behind the City of Santa Barbara have reported seeing the eastern three Channel Islands bathed in bright sunshine while a low fogbank obscured San Miguel.[2] Nonetheless, the island has drama, and its wave-beaten and windy shores are teeming with life.

San Miguel has a unique climate importantly related to its positioning directly to the south of Point Conception. The Point is the most dominant feature of the whole California coast: above it the coast trends north to south, below it the coast trends west to east. Thus, the point protects the whole southerly coast and most of the channel islands from prevailing winds, but not San Miguel. Northwest winds impact forcefully against the Santa Ynez Mountains, sweep around Point Conception increasing in intensity as the channel narrows between the Point and San Miguel Island, and sweep across the island at full force. Whipping up the water, the winds cause strong swells that roll into the channel and send continuous sets of waves breaking relentlessly upon San Miguel's shores. The island's mesa-like form reflects a long history of sea and wind erosion. The northwest winds are believed to date back to the Pleistocene age.

Although the island is 26 miles off Point Conception and 40 miles from Santa Barbara's harbor, until recent times it was difficult to reach. Sailors in the nineteenth century had to approach the island without advance weather reports, and they complained of heavy swells and of having to turn back. Swells whipped up near San Miguel's west end can be felt soon after small craft leave Santa Barbara and they can progressively worsen.

Difficulty of access has contributed an air of isolation and mystery to the island, "mystery" being the key word in the title of many a magazine article describing it. Living there in charge of island ranching so affected two American men that they each dismissed their democratic heritage and claimed to be sovereign kings. The environmentalist's hallmark has taken over now, and we read more about San Miguel's dramatic landscape, wildlife, plants and the history of man's occupation there. For these reasons researchers commonly find it to be their favorite of all the Channel Islands. To the scientist it is a treasure island, a rare microcosm of marine and land environment.

San Miguel Island is about eight miles long, four miles wide, and 10,000 acres in area. Rocks and reefs surround it, and kelp beds as magnificent as redwood forests are anchored to these offshore rocks. The irregular 27 mile coastline bends on the north-central side to a graceful curve. Here, behind the protection of Harris Point and Bat Rock is Cuyler Harbor. Prince Island, 39.4 acres in area and close to 300 feet high, guards its entrance; and the harbor provides protection from southwest storms.

Most of San Miguel's tableland rises abruptly from the sea to about 200 or 300 feet. Green Mountain (817 feet) and San Miguel Hill (831 feet) are two mound-like hills near the middle of the island. A little over six miles northwest of Point Bennett Richardson Rock rises fifty feet from the sea's surface. The desolate tableland above Point Bennett is covered with sand and calcareous deposits but finally gives way to grasses. The slopes lead eastward to Green Mountain and display a wind gap between it and San Miguel Hill where Pleistocene seas once passed. The

Bill Roberts

Prince Island at Cuyler Harbor, a popular spot for Sunday picnics and birds.

island's east end terminates in a sand spit, Cardwell Point. Here the island is separated from Santa Rosa Island by the three mile wide San Miguel Passage.

The World View

San Miguel's isolation has never barred the little island from a role in world, national, or California history. Following centuries of Indian settlement, a Spanish explorer anchored there, restless mountain men arrived in the 1840's to hunt sea mammals, and they together with international ship owners sought oil and fur for world markets. Big lumber schooners risked the seas round San Miguel to bring their cargoes to San Pedro. Ranchers brought out sheep and found both despair and enormous personal satisfaction in the isolation. In more recent times military use, off-shore oil exploitation, and finally National Park protection have made San Miguel Island relevant to modern history. Resembling in some ways the Galapagos Islands off the coast of Ecuador, San Miguel is a natural laboratory where scientists can study the effects of isolation on genetic characteristics.

During its first century under the American flag San Miguel's peculiar location kept its past under cover. Except for the sailor who owned a good seaworthy boat, the associates of ranchers, or small bands of scientific researchers, few really knew or cared about the island. Now, the large number of sturdy private boats in our harbors and National Park status for San Miguel have created an entirely new generation of island watchers. Sports enthusiasts, divers, and tourists from all over the world can visit this secluded outpost. And so it is time to bring together some of what is known about San Miguel. Long overlooked by California historians, its story adds a new chapter to the saga of the golden state. Since human history has a universal appeal, it is presented as Part I. Natural history follows in Part II. The parts may be read in either order, and a reading of the Pleistocene landscape evolution first may have definite advantages for you.

PART I

Chapter II

PREHISTORY: From Collectors To Archaeologists

Archaeologists now believe that people have lived on San Miguel Island either continually or intermittently for over 10,000 years. The singular piece of archaeological evidence that would place it as early as 10,700 years before the present (B.P.) was found at the Daisy Cave site on the eastern end of the island. Since evidence of man's presence on neighboring Santa Rosa Island is clearly dated at 11,000 B.P., this figure is probably correct.[1] This would have been near the beginning of the Holocene Epoch when glacial seas were still on the rise. Prehistoric San Miguel man could have lived on the ancient island Santarosae, then with the rapid sea-level rise and the separation of Santarosae Island into Anacapa, Santa Cruz, Santa Rosa, and San Miguel he could have simply maintained his settlement on the western extremity of the large island. Whether he migrated or lived there continuously, he survived as the ultimate beneficiary of a rich ecosystem that had developed southeast of present-day Point Conception.

North of Point Conception the California Current brought cold water from Alaska down along the North Pacific coast. As it reached Point Conception the flow moved out to the west. The Coriolis or spinning effect of the earth, the shape of the coast formed by Point Conception, and the forces of the California current sucked the water off the California coast. At the same time northwesterly winds blew along the coast and through the Santa Barbara Channel hustling surface waters away from the shore. These phenomena created an upwelling of the cold water from ocean depths of three hundred to five hundred meters. Unlike the seasonal ocean upwellings in some other parts of the world, such as those off the coast of Ecuador and Peru, the upwellings here were and are persistent and provide a dependable year-round supply of nutrients. These nutrients provide food for the kelp, and the huge kelp forests anchored to the rocks off Point Bennett and along the south side of San Miguel island support an entire kelp community of marine life. Phytoplankton feed on the nutrients supplied by the upwelling. The phytoplankton in turn provide food for the minute zooplankton, and these in turn form the chief food supply of young fish. This constantly renewed food supports numerous species of fish, crustaceans, sea mammals, and finally humans.

Dan Gotshall

Kelp forests nourished an ecosystem that included young fish, sea mammals, and ancient man.

Over the years observers, collectors, and finally archaeological scholars have grappled with the task of reconstructing the prehistory of the Santa Barbara Channel mainland and its islands. The first to leave a written record were the Spanish. However, their observations were of the late 18th century cultures and did little to enlighten us of the 10,000 years and more of human habitation prior to that time. Contact with the European led to destruction of the native culture and removal of all remaining Indians from San Miguel Island to the mainland in the early nineteenth century.

About twenty-five years after that event sheep herders came out to the island, but for all we know they took little note of the abandoned villages. Thanks to the tremendous erosion potential, the prehistoric sites, burial places and villages, may have been obliterated. Coast Survey parties made soundings at Cuyler Harbor in 1852, landed on the island in 1858, and after a decade of delay due to the Civil War came again between 1871 and 1874. Survey party members W. G. Harford (1872 and 1873) and William H. Dall (1873-1874) collected Indian artifacts they saw on the surface. Like most collectors of their day neither Harford or Dall was trained in archaeology; but with time on their hands when the weather was too bad to make sightings, they probably took up collecting as an avocation or simply to alleviate boredom. Others were soon aware of relatively easy pickings on San Miguel where the winds shifted the sand daily, blowing away the lighter soil and uncovering graveyards to expose full skeletons. Reports of their rolling about on the surface and being covered the next day by four feet of sand drew a number of serious anthropologists to San Miguel.

The Museum Collectors

Archaeology in the 1870's was simply exploratory and intended mainly to collect artifacts for museums. Also, western anthropologists were in the midst of a massive effort to classify all the peoples of the world in accordance with their physical differences. Hair, skin, and eye color were noted, but most important of all was the size of the cranial cavity. It should come as no surprise, suggested the historian Gary Nash, that all of this effort resulted in the conclusion that the superiority of the white Caucasians could be "scientifically" proven. Perhaps a half dozen collectors came to San Miguel Island before 1880, and they took many hundreds of skeletons and even more crania with them.

Channel Islands National Park

San Miguel Islanders' skulls were taken to Paris and to the Smithsonian Institute.

Paul Schumacher, sponsored by the Smithsonian Institute, did his field work during the week of May 5, 1875. Exposed to grinding sand that was propelled by the prevailing northwest wind, sand that coated their provisions and put out their fires, Schumacher and his three hired men left in heavy seas after only four days. But Schumacher had accomplished much and was delighted with the exposed kitchen middens (refuse heaps) where he had found all sorts of food and preparation debris laid bare and ready for surface collecting. He complained that the amateur curiosity-hunters and Mr. Dall of the Coast Survey had taken the best, but he too collected and plundered in a manner unthinkable in terms of scientific methods used today. While he was exhuming old cemeteries, which he claimed promised the richest reward, he found one which yielded about 250 skeletons plus accompanying artifacts. He had seen the same mortuary and burial methods at coastal Chumash Indian sites, but these were unique: He wrote:

> *The bodies were buried in the kjokkenmoddings [kitchen-middens] because the kitchen refuse offered here the only ground which is firm enough to resist caving, and also to prevent the winds from uncovering the dead, as would occur with loose sand.*[2]

Digging to about six feet, Schumacher and his crew found three to four skeletons in a single grave resting one on another or separated by whale bones (the mainlanders used stone slabs as well as bones), some wrapped in matting, and in some cases accompanied by stone knives and spear points. His collections are stored at the Smithsonian along with a map indicating the locations of the graves.

The Smithsonian in concert with the Department of the Interior next financed clergyman Reverend Stephen Bowers to make collections. Unlike Schumacher, Bowers kept field notes and a journal.[3] Although untrained in the art, Bowers was an educated man; and this in combination with interest was enough in his day to gain him the title of archaeologist. Some of his contemporaries, however, chose to put him down by calling him an ordinary pot hunter. He came to California from Indiana by way of Oregon in 1874 and began to collect archaeological data [material evidence] in the Chumash region to be displayed at the American Centennial Exhibition of 1876. Schumacher and Dall also contributed to that exhibition. At about this time Bowers was approached by Leon de Cessac of the French Scientific Expedition to California. De Cessac and his partner Alphonse Pinart asked Bowers to guide them to the local Indian sites. This alarmed Bowers since he felt that all the Chumash antiquities should remain in the United States. He refused to help and instead speeded up his own request for financing from the Department of the Interior and went out to collect as much as he could before de Cessac could get underway.

Although de Cessac does not mention Bowers by name, and his adversaries may have included Schumacher as well, when he reported upon the contest de Cessac wrote:

> *Meanwhile my researches and their happy result, having awakened the "patriotic" or "interested" touchiness of various sorry souls, notably one of my archaeological competitors, I was forbidden to excavate a very important cemetery in the very town of Santa Barbara....Not content with paralyzing my efforts, my adversaries sought to force to make me leave the mainland and to restrict my researches solely to Santa Cruz Island.*[4]

A French company owned Santa Cruz, so he felt an element of security there and left it for later. De Cessac was afraid that his collections made at any of the other islands might be seized, so he quickly chartered a schooner, boarded his men, and set out for San Miguel Island. He later wrote that he collected a great number of skulls, some skeletons, bone tools, ornaments, and many mortars during his three week stay. De Cessac then went to San Nicholas Island. He took this huge collection back to Paris where it now rests, at least in part, in the Museum of Man. Meanwhile, he had made sure that the United States had no law that forbade the export of Indian relics. It did not. At that time even the Smithsonian refused to sponsor a bill in Congress to prevent their export. Sponsored by the French Ministry of Public Education, de Cessac appears to have been the best prepared of any of the 1870 decade collectors. He had geological knowledge as did Schumacher; but further, in the Alexander Humboldt tradition, he possessed a good foundation in all of the natural sciences.

We can easily follow the trail of Reverend Bowers because he left ample field notes. Taking along a good sized party which included the island sheep rancher Hiram

Mills, he sailed for San Miguel July 23, 1877. High breakers forced them to anchor a mile from shore, so they made various trips in the lifeboat to bring ashore provisions for their three week stay. By digging their way through the sand they managed to get into Mills's house. Bowers explored the entire island and was the first to note that practically the whole island had once been occupied. Shell refuse, principally red and black abalone, convinced him that this had been the Indian's staple food, and he noted that such debris covered hundreds of acres to a depth of 12 or 15 feet. He too could collect specimens laid bare by the wind: mortars, bone implements, fish hooks, bone whistles, and beads manufactured from the Olivella shells so abundant on the island.

A Santa Barbara dentist, Lorenzo Yates, with Louis Dreyfus, and E. L. Doran also made miscellaneous excavations on San Miguel in the 1870s. Collectively they represented the height of the era obsessed with collecting human skulls. They often left the rest of the skeleton and threw back unattractive objects as they thrashed through the kitchen middens and burial places. In general they looked at kitchen middens only when they could not find a cemetery.

Somewhat later in the nineteenth century a few ethnographers, scholars who use early travel journals, church records, and interviews in their research, set about collecting information from the descendents of the Chumash Indians still alive. Leon de Cessac had actually done some work along this line by placing his collections at the foot of State Street, Santa Barbara, and asking the local Chumash descendents to explain to him their use. However, his notes have yet to be located. H. W. Henshaw from the Bureau of American Ethnology and Lorenzo Yates interviewed living informants, but John Peabody Harrison who joined the Smithsonian staff in 1914 contributed even more to this effort. For example, he took down the oral narratives of myth and folklore which circulated among the Chumash people and which greatly helped to explain their social behavior and religious beliefs. One of his informants, Fernando Librado, claimed he was born on Santa Cruz Island, became a cowboy under Hispanic tutelage, and later lived at the Los Cruces stage station near Gaviota. Librado recalled a story in which one of the characters likened the flowers on the islands to the sun itself being on the ground. These would match today's yellow coreopsis. By combining this somewhat sparse ethnographic data with archaeological resources scholars have tried to reconstruct the Chumash life ways of the Late Prehistoric period. However, to find out about prehistoric man who lived on San Miguel Island five or ten thousand years ago would require a greater dependence upon archaeology and paleontology.

The effort to collect materials on San Miguel went ahead as fast as the money to support it was forthcoming. The Heye Foundation in New York sponsored a six month field trip for Ralph Glidden and two assistants in 1919. They were collecting for the Museum of the American Indian, unearthed 343 skeletons and collected thousands of artifacts. These, they felt, they were fortunate to find since Schumacher alone had uncovered, possibly taken, about 250 skeletons in his four days, and every burial site they approached had already been disturbed. Upon completing the field work, and sorting out the data, the Heye Foundation scholars published a monograph entitled *Certain Artifacts from San Miguel Island, California*. It carried research for the island a step further as the brief synthesis below demonstrates.

San Miguel had an oil seepage two miles off the northeast shore that discharged large quantities of asphaltum. Through the action of water and waves globular masses, some weighing several pounds, came ashore. The islanders used it to great advantage in plugging the holes of the abalone shell, as a cement for fish hooks, in attaching knife handles, and as a substance in which to embed shells when making ornaments.

The Foundation catalogued, photographed, and analyzed the use of hundreds of artifacts. They found mortars made from large pecked beach pebbles and used for heating asphaltum or as paint cups. Glidden surmised that the soap stone (steatite) cooking vessels were made from mainland stone, as there was no steatite on San Miguel. He saw ornamented stone sinkers, curved fish hooks, and bones made into a myriad of useful artifacts: needles, pins, whistles, beads, pendants, and arrow points. Shells, especially the abalone *haliotis,* were used for every purpose. Equally common in the burial places and elsewhere was the *Olivella biplicata,* a shell measured in pecks and appearing in quantities of up to 6,000 in a single grave. Glidden's findings produced a virtual encyclopedia of San Miguel's artifacts. He gave much space to mortuary habits and was impressed with the important part bone played in the life of the people. Regarding ocean travel he wrote:

> *The very life of the Chumash of San Miguel depended on their ability to leave their limited domain at will, and the description by early voyagers of their well-built canoes with their long paddles, so skillfully and powerfully used, leaves no doubt as to their means of communication with adjacent islands and the mainland. It is therefore to be regretted that no example of the only means of transportation which the islanders possessed has been found.*[5]

David Banks Rogers made two one-day visits to the island in 1927 while collecting material for his work *Prehistoric Man of the Santa Barbara Coast.* He echoed Bowers when he wrote, "We have here the remains of the most extensive unbroken Indian settlement, of which we have knowledge, on the American continent north of the Mexican boundary."[6] He decried the 1870 mania for collecting curios. Rogers wrote that abalone shells were present in tons and fish and seal bones too. It appeared that the islanders resource base, although limited in variety, was very dependable. Fish and sea mammals could be caught in every season. Did the life of the people ever depend upon their ability to leave San Miguel as Glidden had suggested? As long as their springs did not run dry, was there any reason barring a natural catastrophe that they could not live indefinitely from the resources of the sea?

Archaeology Comes of Age

Gradually attention began to shift away from collecting artifacts and towards establishing cultural chronology. Archaeologists began systematic excavations in the stratum at many levels on the neighboring island of Santa Rosa in 1933 and to define a sequence of cultures spanning the thousands of years of occupancy. No archaeological work had been done on San Miguel Island for over twenty years when Phil C. Orr of the Santa Barbara Museum of Natural History inventoried some sites in 1950, and introduced carbon dating. He was followed in the 1960's by Charles Rozaire of the Los Angeles Museum of Natural History who provided the base for nearly all our current understanding of prehistoric life on the island. George Kritzman directed the survey work between 1964 and 1966, and his teams ultimately covered the whole island numbering, mapping, and filling out forms for some 524 sites. Rozaire selected a few sites to excavate based upon their undisturbed condition and upon their relative depth and began to reconstruct the chronology. He used the Schumacher and Heye Foundation maps to correlate his locations.

Still in 1978 there were only nine radio carbon dates from San Miguel, and none pertained to excavated collections. With the advent of environmental laws in the 1970s the federal government was committed to an active role in saving and managing cultural resources, so in 1976 the National Park Service asked Dr. Michael A. Glassow to provide an update on the status of the island's archaeological sites. A flurry of activity followed. Notably, archaeologists Phillip Walker, Steve Craig, Roberta Greenwood and Pandora Smethkamp have led survey and excavation teams to San Miguel, and ethnographers John Johnson and Chester King have brought our understanding to new heights.[7]

For example, we now know that during the entire prehistoric period, that is until the advent of the Spanish, San Miguel's inhabitants lived mainly along the north side of the island. Since a steep coastal bluff characterizes the south shoreline, the northern shore would naturally have afforded easier access to intertidal zones. Also, today and possibly then, nearly all the fresh water sources are located on the north side of the island. Prehistoric sites indicating habitation were found clustered on the western part of the island on small coastal bluffs 50-150 feet above sea level and on the broad plateau 200-350 feet above sea level. The latter would have demanded greater effort in transporting marine food and driftwood with which to build their fires, but there would have been less blowing sand and the view was magnificent. The view also could have afforded warning of intruders; and as material evidence has shown, there was violence. Apparently there was no major difference in activities at the various locations since the cemeteries, craft items, and kitchen trash heaps at both were just about the same.[8]

Reaching back over the millenniums in search of some kind of time marker for prehistoric chronology, archaeologist Chester King found a key in the ways by which a certain shell had been modified and remodified. This is discussed below. The periods King set down have been widely used by other scholars and are as follows: Early Period (7,000 B.C. to 1400 B. C.), Middle Period (1400 B.C. to A.D 1050), and Late Period (A.D. 1050 to 1782).[9]

The rolling terrain of San Miguel did not provide a habitat for trees and plants such as those found on Santa Cruz and Santa Rosa Islands. Although the plant life was probably more diverse in earlier times, before stripping by the Pleistocene pigmy elephant and before nineteenth century sheep grazing, prehistoric man could not have subsisted solely from the sources he found on land. He had always looked to the sea. Pandora Smethkamp assembled the best picture we have yet of prehistoric foods and how they varied throughout time after she excavated several archaeological sites in the 1980's. By clearing away vertical profiles at the sites, mapping and numbering the different strata, taking column samples, and bagging the soils and faunal remains, she had the raw material evidence to take back to a mainland laboratory for screening, intensive analysis and dating.

Smethkamp's excavation at Daisy Cave brought unexpected results. For the first time on San Miguel the samples yielded dates ranging from 3,430 Before the Present (B.P.) clear back to 10,260 B.P. The faunal remains revealed that the primary sources of protein in the early Holocene Epoch, about 8,000 B.P. to 10,260 B.P., were some upper intertidal mollusks, the *Tegula funebralis* and *Mytilus californianus*. These two species alone accounted for over 85 percent of the mass of shellfish remains in the kitchen middens. Found under exposed rocks at low tide they could have been taken by hand or by a trap pulled from the shore. Fish, wintering birds such as the Arctic loon and flightless duck *Chendytes lawli,* and an occasional sea mammal rounded out the protein diet. Apparently, a small group of people had occupied Daisy Cave during the winter gathering shellfish, netting or snaring birds, and taking fish from near the shore using lines attached to small bipointed fishhooks. Why they took so few sea mammals is not known. The pinniped (fin-footed marine mammals) preceded man in the Pacific Ocean here having evolved by the early Pliocene and migrated into the North Pacific at least a million and a half years ago. Perhaps the pinnipeds were not actively hauling out or breeding on San Miguel during this Early Period.[10]

Later on in King's Early Period (circa 8,000, B.P. to 6,450, B.P.) prehistoric man made a significant shift in his diet. A red abalone, the *Haliotis rufescens,* dominated very large middens. Glassow found these red abalone sites all along the northern and southern shorelines and especially at Harris Point. Glassow suggested that sea water temperatures were about two degrees lower than our modern water temperatures and that this could account for the abundance of these red abalones. They flourish at such water temperatures. Still, in certain samples ninety percent of the shells continued to be from intertidal mollusks.

Sea mammal hunting suddenly appeared to be an important strategy between 4,350 B.P. and 3,350 B.P. becoming firmly established during King's late Early Period. Specialized tools to snare and extract game appeared such as shell fishhooks, stone projectile points of exotic cherts, (flat flint-like rocks) and bone tools. With the waning of the Early Period diverse shellfish predominated in the diet while the red abalone almost disappeared and was no longer present anywhere as the predominant species.

During the Middle Period the inhabitants took a variety of sea mammals, a high proportion of which were young adults and the most common being the Guadalupe fur seal. Archaeologists Walker and Craig identified the remains of the California sea lion, Stellar sea lion, Northern fur seal, northern elephant seal, harbor seal, and the sea otter dating to the earliest part of the Middle Period.[11] The slow moving

William Bryan

The prehistoric San Miguelenos captured many sea otters.

pinniped at his rookery could be taken with a tool no more elaborate than a club. The superabundance of food during the pinniped breeding season lent a seasonal pulse to the islanders' diet. Sea birds decreased in importance. Paleontologist Guthrie has suggested that birds may have been taken primarily for skins rather than for meat. Thus as sea mammals with their high-quality furs were hunted, the need for birds may have decreased. Fish remains such as the surfperch indicated that fishing was still confined to rocky inshore and sandy inshore habitats, but in the transition to the Late Period rockfish declined in importance.

Fishing in the Late Period infrequently took place in the outer kelp beds and open waters. While it is known that Channel Island Indians did develop fishhooks to take large fish from their sea-going canoes, there is little evidence of these large pelagic fish in the middens at San Miguel. Such fishhooks were made of two symmetrical pieces of bone used to make a bipointed hook shaped much like our own fish hooks. The two bones were wrapped together with a cord and fastened with asphaltum.

In the Late Period the sea mammal played an important role. Charles Rozaire examined the faunal remains recovered from an excavation above the present sea rookery at Point Bennett. Some of the deposits there represented Indian occupation dating from about a thousand years ago. The remains of the Guadalupe fur seal were the most abundant of those found even though the fur seals are not numerous today. The remains of sea otters were so numerous as to suggest that this site functioned as a camp for prehistoric otter hunters. More otter bones occurred at the bottom of the excavation than at the top. Phillip Walker examined the site and noting the distribution of sea otter bones, he compared it to a prehistoric Aleut site. At that Aleut site overexploitation of sea otters had "caused a disruption of the kelp bed ecosystem and destruction of the rich fauna of fish, birds, and marine mammals the kelp beds once supported."[12] Still, it is up to speculation as to whether the otter off San

Miguel became scarce thanks to overexploitation or for some other reason such as a change in oceanographic conditions.

Plants were probably important food sources as well for the prehistoric Indians. The grasslands would have supplied edible roots, tubers, and seeds. The *Brodiaea sp*, for example, provided a bulb to roast. When the Heye Foundation sent out its collectors to San Miguel, they found many donut-shaped stones that are know to have been used as digging stick weights. Sage seeds also could have been an important nutritional item. Plant foods were not abundant, and the San Miguel Islander may have had a hard time achieving a balanced diet. Skulls examined show that he had a high incidence of *Cribia orbitalia,* a condition in which porous bone develops in the roofs of the cranial orbits. This deformity is associated with anemia produced either by infections, diarrhea, or a parasite infestation and thus suggests ongoing health problems. Further, his diet lacked fibrous terrestrial plant foods, and he ate mainly soft fish and sea mammal meat. This could have caused a periodontal disease believed to have been prevalent on the island.[13]

The limited resources may have led to disputes and help explain a high incidence of traumatic injuries. Life was probably more severe on San Miguel than on any of the other Channel Islands. The islanders kept dogs as pets, as guardians against intruders, and perhaps too as emergency food. Feeding dogs excess food in times of abundance and eating them at times of food shortage would have fit the life of the San Miguel Islander, dependent as he was upon the marine environment and the shortage of plant foods.[14]

Trade and Crafts

Some of the older deposits revealed that the islanders were crafting bipointed bone gorges, barrel shaped shell beads from the *Olivella biplicata,* and cordage as early as 8000 B.P. Since steatite and obsidian were not present on San Miguel, it is assumed that when artifacts made from these exotic materials appeared in the middens inter-island or mainland trade was taking place. The Heye Foundation collectors recovered ornaments, bowls, and exotic obsidian projection points that have been dated to the early Middle Period. As pinnipeds became more common in the diet, their bones were fashioned as flakers and other bone tools useful for working hides. Fragments of whale bones suggest that the islanders used whale bone for cemetery markers as did the mainlanders.[15]

Rising seas and the separation of the ancient Santarosae Island into the four northern Channel Islands would have prompted the need for reliable boat transportation for inter-island and mainland trade and for communication. No pieces of plank canoes have yet been found on San Miguel. Nor did Cabrillo report upon any canoes. Sebastian Vizcaino who sailed among the Channel Islands in 1602 left the only written record of a San Miguel canoe. His party saw it in December and wrote:

> *A canoe came out with two Indians and a small boy, their eyes being painted with antimony. They asked us to go to their land; however, there was such a heavy sea and the island presented so many shoals that we did not dare to go, but veered out to sea.*[16]

Lacking their own trees, these islanders could have fashioned their canoes from driftwood, but they probably bought their canoes. For the bulk of their transport they could have depended upon wealthy canoe owners from Santa Rosa Island or from the mainland trading center of Shisholop, at Refugio.

Trade changed their lives, of course, and opened up a chance to manufacture goods in great demand on the mainland. Into their lives may have come seeds, steatite from Catalina Island, heavy stone metates on which they could grind dried meat, planks, large baskets, and Yucca bulbs. One late Middle Period site studied included a stratum that indicated a specialized production of stone bowls and pestles.[17] Although it is doubtful that these were for export, sea mammal body parts, sea otter skins, and shell beads were surely commodities they could offer to mainland trade.

Market demand or cultural preference may account for the frequency with which the Guadalupe fur seal was butchered. Just as we select our filet mignons, the Indian butchered in favor of heavily muscled parts, the meaty forearms. In otariids, such as the fur seal, the forelimbs are the main locomotor organs and contain approximately 30 percent of the body's total muscle mass. As the distance from the Point Bennett rookery increased, the greater was the likelihood of finding only the forearm bones in the trash heaps. Instead of carrying an entire seal carcass overland, it made sense to carry just the meaty cuts. Even in mainland middens many miles from any rookery, only the forearm bones would be present. The same rationale would carry over to trade as cargo space in the plank boat was limited.[18]

William F. Bryan

Clothing made of the otter's fur was a status symbol among some Indians and a valuable trade item.

Chester King's ethnographic research disclosed that Indians who lived on Santa Rosa Island traded sea otter pelts to people living on the mainland during the historic period, so San Miguel Islanders probably did the same and in the prehistoric period.[19] Otters were killed for their fur, a fur used to make bed covers, arrow quivers, and clothing. Otter skins were a status symbol. In Northern California the Indians had laws regarding clothing and social class that paralleled Spanish law: otter skin apparel like the European silks and taffetas was forbidden for use by common people. The common Indian was punished for even hunting the otter.[20]

San Miguel's greatest source of income undoubtedly came from the manufacture of shell-derived coins (currency). The finished product was a bead which could be strung or stored in baskets. Beads were the standard for money, as we know it, the measurement based upon length of strand or volume. As the trade network expanded, demand grew, and by the eighteenth century the San Miguelenos were so trade oriented they probably would have found it extremely difficult to have reverted to a simple subsistence way of life.

The *Olivella biplicata,* a small spire and base univalve shell common in the Channel and thus to San Miguel, was crafted and modified and used as currency throughout the southern part of California and east to the Colorado River for up to 4,000 years. Archaeologist Chester King studied changes in the modifications made upon the shell, and it was while doing this that he realized that it could serve as a time marker. For example, at the Early Period the spires were commonly removed, or the spire and base, or the shell reduced to a rectangle. During the Middle Period the spire was ground diagonally or the shell reduced to a disc or saucer. In the Late Period cupped beads were made from the chert area of the shell. As bead sources King used burial sites, camp sites, and debris middens that archaeologists had studied on the mainland and on Santa Cruz Island. He did this because research had progressed so much further at those locations.

Beads have been collected both on the surface and in excavations on San Miguel. Crews have found shells reduced to discs, others with the spire lopped off. These modifications indicated two types of manufacture, types significant of two distant time periods: the disc from about 1500 years ago and the latter type from much earlier. Until further research on San Miguel can be undertaken, we must borrow from findings about the Chumash culture at large, knowing that this island was a component of it.

The clam, mussel, and abalone shell also lent themselves to bead manufacture, an occupation that no doubt kept many islanders busy all of the day. The Chumash used these beads as a display of wealth. One young girl, a dog-girl in a myth and married to a chief's son, was dressed in a many-stranded necklace, a bracelet, earrings, a basket-hat, and an otter skin apron.

With the advent of Cabrillo's voyage, (see Chapter 3), glass beads made in Venice appeared along the Santa Barbara Channel. Upon Spanish settlement in the late eighteenth century glass beads rapidly replaced the shells both as an item of conspicuous consumption and as a medium of exchange. Spanish observers wrote that the Chumash would trade anything, even their canoes, in order to get the beads. The businesslike Chumash created a scale of values for the glass beads. Longinos Martinez observed that glass value depended upon fineness, color, time in circulation, and number in circulation.

King found that as soon as the glass beads came into circulation, the manufacture of Olivella cupped and lipped beads ended. The economy on San Miguel probably suffered a collapse. On the heels of the glass bead crisis came the absorbtion of the mainland population into the missions and the end to the great trade network which had for centuries created a demand for their bead product. Also, to make matters worse, there were the foreign fur-hunters. Ethnographer John Johnson suggests that with all of these setbacks the islanders may have been willing to leave their homes and accept conversion on the mainland. However we may assess their leaving, it was a tragedy. Limited resources from which to live, incessant winds and blowing sand were always stark realities. Still, for those who knew the island year around and for all of their lives it could have been the center of the earth, and the best of all places.

Prehistoric Impact upon the Island's Ecology

If prehistoric man inhabited the island for ten thousand years or more, we might ask in what ways did his presence change the island's ecology. Some evidence suggests that fires started by prehistoric man destroyed plant life, but we cannot really know. A pygmy elephant known to inhabit the island apparently disappeared at about the time human predators appeared on the island, but until we find conclusive evidence, such as a spear point stuck in an elephant bone, we cannot connect man to its extinction for sure either. A flightless duck coexisted with man over several thousands of years and then disappeared from the record. The island fox survived the entire Indian period of occupancy.

Even when choice sea mammal meat was traded externally, it is almost certain that the Indian's exploitation of these sea mammals resulted in no marked interference with their natural pattern of activities. We had no pinniped population counts till the 1920's, and in the 1980's 15 to 20 thousand animals hauled up on San Miguel's beaches. The prehistoric numbers may well have been greater, quite a figure to destabilize if butchering was done with flat flint-like rock tools rather than steel knives and if transport of their meat depended upon canoes. The period of real mass chaos for these mammals came as a result of world demand for their oil and furs in the late nineteenth century and a hunt to extinction. This, the white man's hunt, is treated ahead.

The popular view of prehistoric Indians as "prudent predators" may be placed under scrutiny at San Miguel in the case of otter hunting. Among the Aleutian Islanders overexploitation of sea otters caused a disruption in an entire kelp bed ecosystem. In spite of the heavy population on the Santa Barbara Channel mainland, Walker found sea otter bones much more common in San Miguel Island middens than along the coast. This may have been because the large Chumash villages on the coast had simply reduced the size of their otter populations. Another explanation for this would be the relatively nutrient rich water at San Miguel that made it a productive otter habitat. However, since many more otter remains were at the bottom than at the top of the excavation near Point Bennett, this raises the question of a depletion of otters simply to satisfy a subsistence or trade bias. Man is the otter's only serious predator, and prehistoric man hunted it for the fur, not the meat.

Several writers have challenged the view of the wise Indian who lived and consciously worked for a balanced relationship with the plants and animals he exploited. Daniel Guthrie wrote:

> *The Indian's actions toward nature were, and are identical to those of modern man. What concern for the environment there was existed for the expressed purpose of guaranteeing human survival. A true reverence for nature, where nonhuman organisms are given a right to survival equal to that of man, had never been part of man's emotional makeup. Man shares with all other animals a basic lack of concern about his effect on his surroundings....Man's attitude toward the environment has not changed in the millennia since his evolution from lower animals. Only his population size and the sophistication of his technology are different.*[21]

We can learn more about prehistoric man on San Miguel Island. The material evidence located in the archaeological sites is all we have to work from. After a hundred years of pot hunting the task of excavation and analysis has really just begun. Wind and weather have long jumbled and uncovered cultural debris, and on the western end of the island and near Point Bennett the pinnipeds are presently destroying the Indian middens as they haul out. Thus, an urgency exists. On the other hand, the island's isolation has helped. Comparable to regions on the adjacent coastal mainland, there are many more sites completely intact. There are deep sites with sharply stratified deposits because there have been no burrowing animals to disturb them. Glassow writes, " It would be no exaggeration to say that the [Northern Channel] islands' archaeological resources should be considered as some of the most valuable on the west coast of North America."[22]

These sites must be carefully protected against modern pot hunters and even hikers who do not realize how devastating any disturbance to sites can be to their research potential. New laboratory and excavation techniques are being developed and these lead to new methods to apply to the evidence that is there. Archaeologists of the next century will be better equipped to understand the historic meaning of the fragments of bone and shell than any of our present-day experts. When the National Park Service closes off parts of the island to visitation or insists that visitors be accompanied by rangers and to stay on the trails, it is not only protecting plants and insects—the Park Service is saving archaeological material for yet unborn archaeologists and paleontologists.

Chapter III

VOYAGES OF EXPLORATION

Juan Rodriguez Cabrillo, An Historical Update

Spain's great *siglo de oro* was half gone when Captain Juan Rodriguez Cabrillo led three ships north out of Puerto de Navidad on the west coast of New Spain on June 27, 1542. He had orders to search along the coast of Alta California for a northwest passage, to make settlements if the country were good, and to discover riches for Spain. Christopher Columbus had failed to find a passage to the East, and Hernando Cortes and the first wave of grand conquistadores had either died or returned to Spain. On this epic voyage Cabrillo fell short of completing his tasks, but he did reach the California coast and was the first to bring San Miguel Island into recorded history. When his tattered ships returned to the port of Navidad nine months later Cabrillo was dead as were several of the crew, and all of the expensive trade goods he had taken along were lost.

The economic disaster of that expedition prompted the Royal Audiencia, a judicial and administrative body, to send a notary to Navidad where he was to gather the facts and write up a report. Juan Leon did this, writing a summary which mainly brought together interviews with crew members he met and segments of the captain's log. His work was handed about, condensed, copied and recopied. As a result it, and the historical works which depended upon it, suffered from distortions. Some people even mistook it for the actual ship's log. There would be no reason to include here all of this detail about Juan Leon's summary or "log," or even to highlight Juan Cabrillo's voyage were it not for the long-held assumption that Cabrillo was a Portugese and had died on San Miguel. These old concepts have recently been challenged by Cabrillo's biographer, Harry Kelsey.[1]

Supplementing the Leon summary with testimony gathered from court records, historic maps and bundles of documents at the Spanish archives, he presented a whole new concept of Cabrillo's stay at the California Islands.

Recapitulating Kelsey's work, let us begin with the erroneously-held concept that Juan Rodriguez, was a Portugese. He probably had no family name to claim upon birth, or during the time he grew up in the environs of Seville. Apparently he added the surname Cabrillo when he reached the New World. In the late sixteenth century the Royal Spanish historian, Antonio de Herrera, compiled a history of Spain and used Leon's summary. In it, and for the first time, he referred to Cabrillo as a Portuguese. Thus, for centuries Cabrillo was called a Portuguese. But many historians today are convinced he was a Spaniard. Portuguese pilots were in high regard in the sixteenth century, and a pilot and captain on the voyage named Antonio Correa was indeed a Portuguese. Perhaps Herrera made an error while copying or revising his manuscript placing the word Portuguese after Cabrillo's name by mistake. Research has shown that Cabrillo or even Cabrilho are not and probably never were Portuguese names!

The Spanish Cabrillo made his way to the New World as a youth just in time to serve in the bloody task of taking Cuba. The slaughter of thousands of natives there undoubtedly made Cabrillo a good crossbowman, a pragmatic leader, and strengthened his convictions of racial superiority. Learning ship building along the way he followed his leader Panfilo de Narvaez to mainland New Spain where as a reward for his part in its conquest he received land, free Indian labor in the form of *encomiendas,* and slaves in the Captaincy General of Guatemala. Growing rich from his cacao plantations, mining operations, and trade, he abandoned a liaison he had with an Indian woman, brought a Spanish wife to New Spain, and became a local official.

Cabrillo was a notch above the average ex-soldier, and at about forty years old was appointed by the frontier governor, Pedro de Alvarado, to take charge of the nearby shipyard, Iztapa. Alvarado and his partner, Viceroy

Mendoza of New Spain, were building a fleet at Iztapa for both private gain and exploration. Between 1536 and 1540 Cabrillo built seven or eight ships, pouring his fortune into a galleon of his own. Cabrillo had ample experience in the administration of slave labor at his private mines and plantations, and he joined with Alvarado in making the most of Indian labor near the port. The priest, Bartolome de Las Casas, wrote of how the Indians were forced to carry four-hundred pound anchors and other materials from the east coast of the Captaincy General of Guatemala to the west and how women and girls were herded onto the ships to satisfy the soldiers and sailors. Men of Cabrillo's station felt it only proper to depopulate villages to promote their enterprise. In spite of laws on the books to the contrary, this mentality and the penchant to treat Indians as expendable property were mindsets bound to instruct Cabrillo and his men when they made their landings on the Channel Islands off California.

Cabrillo took Alvarado's fleet north to a port he named Navidad in December, 1540, but before any ships could be dispatched for exploration Alvarado was killed in an Indian uprising. His partner, Viceroy Mendoza, took command sending some ships to the Spice Islands and Juan Rodriguez Cabrillo to California. Cabrillo's small armada was composed of his own galleon, the *San Salvador* but also called *Juan Rodriguez* and *Capitana;* another galleon, *La Victoria;* and a small brigantine, the *San Miguel,* which was useful in ferrying men and cargo from ship to shore. As the ships traveled up the coast of Baja California they sailed north of waters and land never before claimed for Spain. This was true even though the explorers Francisco de Ulloa in 1539 and Francisco de Bolanos in 1540 had established that Baja California was a peninsula.[2] Cabrillo went ashore to claim possession for the Kingdom of Spain at numerous bays and points of land, naming these landmarks after feast days with which the discovery coincided, after their ships, or he simply called the place La Posesion. Thus, in reading of La Posesion in Leon's summary one could attach it to any of a number of places.

Cabrillo referred to all of the Channel Islands as the San Lucas Islands. He named his headquarters island, our Santa Catalina Island of today, after his ship, the *San Salvador*. Thus in the ship's log, Catalina took on all the ship's other names, and was also called La Posesion. The last would contribute importantly to disinformation accepted until very recently about San Miguel Island's identity and history.

On October 18, 1542 Cabrillo's fleet attempted to round Point Conception and met head on with the prevailing northwest winds. It turned back and conveniently found refuge "at the smaller of two islands" close by in the outer ocean. Juan Leon's "log" states that they remained on the islands until the following Wednesday because there was a violent storm."[3] Cabrillo may have gone ashore in the traditional manner to take possession of San Miguel for the King of Spain and even have made contact with the Indians there. He apparently called the island La Posesion. The "log" describes a good port and villages on this smaller of the "two islands," and continues that all the ships took their departure from it when the storm abated. The ships may have anchored for that week in Cuyler Harbor. All sorts of things could have happened. We can only guess. Kelsey estimates that close to 250 people were aboard: crew, soldiers, slaves, and at least one priest, Fray Julian de Lescano, and perhaps women.

People may have wanted to get off those ships and go ashore. Climbing the steep canyon up from Cuyler Harbor must not have been as attractive or as easy as stepping out onto neighboring Santa Rosa Island.

In 1901 an archaeologist found a stone on Santa Rosa Island marked JRC and that has since set off a great deal of guessing.

The log recites that on Wednesday, the 25th, they left the island farthest to the windward, the one they named Posesion. Surely then, on this day they were at San Miguel and set out from there for the North. Encountering gale force winds they stayed well out to sea, but in due time they sighted Point Reyes and the mouth of the Russian

River. Returning, they passed Point Conception on November 23 and took immediate refuge at Cuyler Harbor. The small brigantine was hauled ashore for repair. Whether the crew walked around the island or met with the Indians is not known. Every man may have been occupied with the task of repair. The brigantine probably joined the other ships at Cabrillo's headquarters, Catalina Island, as soon as possible. As is well known, Cuyler Harbor is not really safe in the winter, the heavy seas causing ships to drag anchor. While earlier readings of the summary "log" led historians to believe that the whole fleet and the some 250 people spent the winter at San Miguel, Kelsey can quote members of the crew who recalled with certainty that the galleons wintered at Catalina Island. Cabrillo's map documented this. The earlier mixup is easily attributed to the fact that both Catalina and San Miguel were called La Posesion. But to winter 250 people on San Miguel when other choices were at hand is, of course, preposterous.

Catalina was not a happy option either. Crew member Francisco de Vargas recalled that all the time the fleet was there, the Indians never stopped fighting them. The little Cabrillo armada had enjoyed a glorious welcome at their first landing on Catalina in early October. What had they done to anger the Indians? Had they mistreated the Indians there and on San Miguel as well? Had they helped themselves to the Indian women? Vargas did not elaborate. Near Christmas a party of men went ashore, were attacked and outnumbered, so Cabrillo led reinforcements ashore to help in the rescue. According to Vargas, Cabrillo broke a shin bone on a rocky ledge as he jumped from a shore boat. Carried back to his ship, he was treated unsuccessfully, and gangrene set in. When death neared Cabrillo ordered his pilot, Bartolome Ferrer, to complete the voyage. The Capitana died January 3, 1543.

If Cabrillo was buried on an island, that island was La Capitana or today's Santa Catalina. In 1937 and on the 394th anniversary of Juan Rodriguez Cabrillo's death, the Cabrillo Civic Clubs of California placed a monumental granite cross on a knoll overlooking the harbor at San Miguel Island. It commemorated Cabrillo as a Portuguese, "Jaoa R. Cabrilho," and marked San Miguel as the place of his burial. It is now the most prominent structure on the island. Unfortunately, it commemorates an earlier era of historical misunderstanding.

Mike Maki

The Cabrillo Cross overlooking Cuyler Harbor, a monument to historical misunderstanding.

The Pilot Ferrer guided the fleet north to about 44 degrees latitude, and the three ships returned to Navidad, New Spain April 14, 1543. Cabrillo's men had probably seen the last of San Miguel Island when the brigantine stopped off there for repairs in November of 1542. Spanish officials in Mexico City were not impressed with the results of the exploration. Cartographers in Seville did not even update their maps to include Upper California's coast for seventeen years.

The confusion over San Miguel Island's history began with Cabrillo, when he named the island La Posesion, the same name he had already used for his headquarter island, today's Catalina Island. Catalina was so important that it was named after Cabrillo's own ship, the *San Salvador*, and then referred to as both *Capitana* and as *Juan Rodriquez*. Not only did translators and historians err in concluding that the return in late 1542 to La Posesion and wintering there meant a return to San Miguel, but they also attached other names used for the headquarter island to San Miguel Island. Kelsey has clearly established that Cabrillo's ships wintered on the first La Posesion, Catalina Island. This new interpretation certainly diminishes San Miguel Island's association with Cabrillo's life and death and with his voyage of exploration.

The Manila Galleon: Searching for a California Port of Call

The report about Cabrillo's discovery of California was so disappointing to the Spanish that they refused to sponsor settlement for over two hundred years. Riches lay in mines and in the Manila Galleon trade begun in 1564. Galleons brought silks and ivories from China by way of the Philippines to New Spain and gained profits of 400 percent on the cargo. The hold and even the deck were packed solid, leaving little space for food and water for the crew. The return trip brought the galleons east to the northern California coast at about Cape Mendocino, and from here they sailed southward to the home port of Acapulco. The four- to six-month journey made the galleons prey to English-based pirates on the last leg and held out a good chance of scurvy for the crew. Mortality became frightful. The *Capitana* of 1629 lost 105, and two galleons a few years later threw overboard 140 persons.

The Spanish decided they needed a port-of-call along California's coast, so select galleon captains reconnoitered the coast on their trip home. Thus, after a lapse of over forty years Spanish ships neared San Miguel Island, but neither Captain Francisco Gali's log of 1584 or that of Pedro de Unamuno in 1587 mentioned it. Disaster struck when Sebastian Rodriguez Cermeno sailed too close to land, and he wrecked his galleon north of San Francisco Bay in 1595. His half-starved men assembled a knocked down launch and continued their close survey of the California coast in the open boat. Cermeno sighted San Miguel Island and the other Channel Islands but did not stop on any of them. Cermeno's log described San Miguel as "a small island which runs northwest and southeast..." and Santa Rosa and Santa Cruz Islands as "bare and sterile, although inhabited by Indians."[5]

Cermeno's catastrophe persuaded Viceroy Monterey to send the next coastal explorer north from Mexico rather than to risk another galleon loaded with oriental luxury goods. In 1603 he equipped Sebastian Vizcaino, a pearl fishing concessionaire, with three ships, directing him to sail back and forth along the coast. Setting out from the tip of Baja California Vizcaino encountered strong northwest winds and made four tries before he finally rounded Cabo San Lucas, reached the Isla de Cedros, and continued north. Sailing back and forth along the coast he did away with many of the names Cabrillo had given to the islands and to points along the coast, changed them, and added new ones. He wrote of the rocky islet northwest of San Miguel Island as the Farallon de Lobos in his log, yet on his plan or map it appears as the Isla de Bajos (Isla de Baxos). It is now known as Richardson Rock. A farallon is a small rocky island.

San Miguel Island on the sailing plan is labeled "S. Anicleto" but never mentioned in the ship's journal. San Anicleto's day is July 14, and Vizcaino's ship the *San Diego* was near San Miguel Island on December 5, 1603. Why he called it S. Ancleto is a mystery. It happened that a canoe with two Indians came out, evidently to greet them.[6]

Vizcaino was so thorough that he sailed to Cape Mendocino, spent eight months at sea, ran short on supplies, and returned to Navidad with half of his crew dead. Scurvy took most of the lives, and no cause or cure for scurvy was to be known for another 150 years at the least. Vizcaino named Monterey Bay in honor of the Viceroy of New Spain and described it as an excellent sheltered harbor. This brought an end to the coastal surveys, but in spite of all this effort few galleons even paused at Monterey. By the time they reached that part of the California coast, they were too near home to bother with a stop.

After 1603 Spain ignored California until the King's Visitador-General Jose de Galvez organized a task force of Church and military personnel to settle it in 1769. Miguel Costanso, an army engineer who marched north with Captain Gaspar de Portola's party, was the next to make a record of San Miguel. He wrote of it as a discovery and named it San Bernardo.[7]

In 1793 the Englishman, George Vancouver, observed San Miguel and placed it on a map he was constructing. This map had lasting impact since it was published in England, then the world center of navigation. Vancouver studied Spanish charts he had brought along, and from one of them he simply chose the name San Miguel.[8] The Frenchman, Duflot de Mofras, followed Vancouver's precedent in the 1840's, so finally the island had a permanent name.[9]

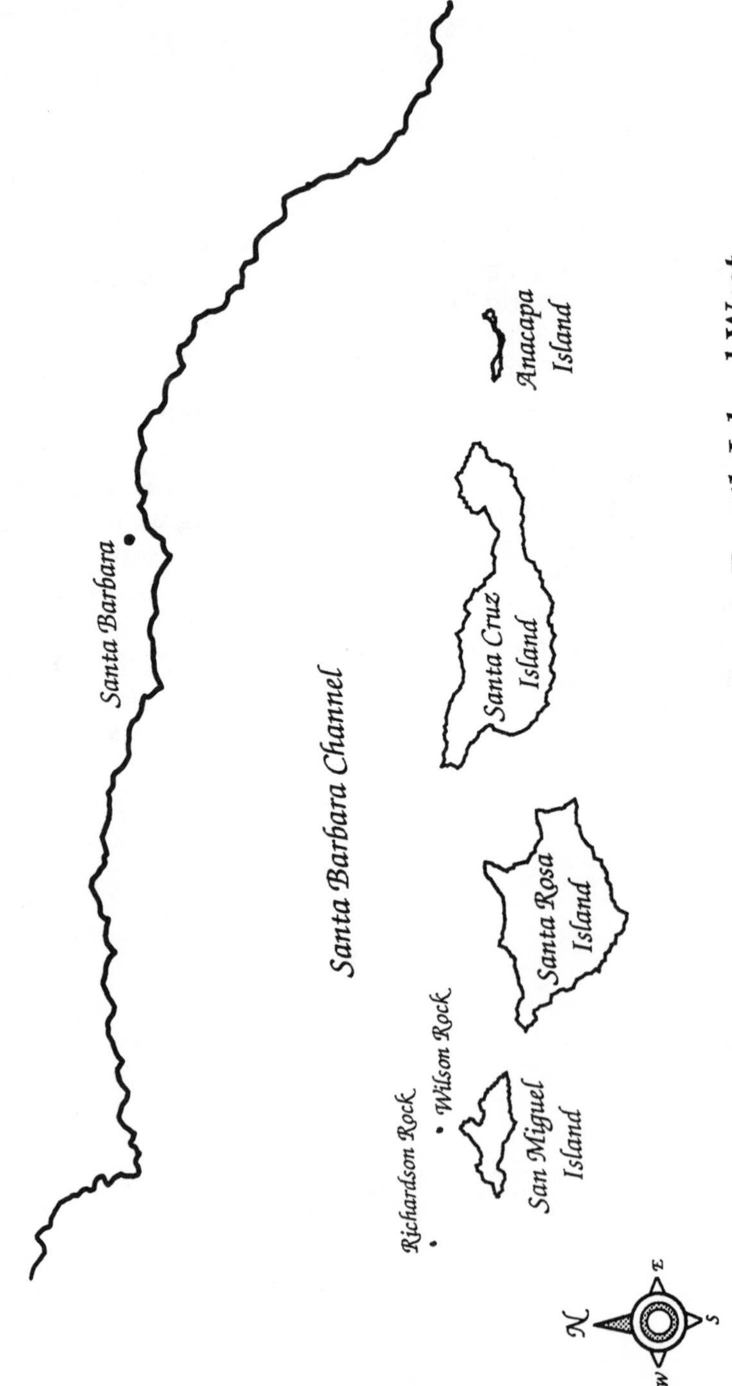

San Miguel Island, Santa Barbara's Fourth Island West

Chapter IV

THE CHUMASH AND THE SPANISH RECORD

The first Spaniards the San Miguel islanders saw were those aboard the three ships of Juan Rodriguez Cabrillo. After this excitement in the Channel they had probably lived on undisturbed until well after the Spanish came north from New Spain to settle Upper California in 1769. At this time they were considered a part of the extensive Chumash culture.

The Spanish Record

The Spanish wrote things down thus creating the first historic record of the Chumash. They sent home descriptive journals treating with the landscape and with social habits and kept track of individuals in their Church archives. Using these sources ethnographers have reached the conclusion that some 3,252 people lived on the four Channel Islands in 1782.[1] Since no effort had been made to bring the islanders to the mainland missions prior to that date, we may guess that this figure was about the same in 1769. Like the Spanish culture, whose seventeenth century institutions had evolved slowly and where their ancestors reached back to a simple stone age culture, the eighteenth century culture along the Santa Barbara Channel called the Chumash had passed through many phases of development. By 1769 it exhibited a complex political and social system and a thriving trade network which reached from the outer off-shore islands eastward to present-day New Mexico.

During the Spanish era in California the Franciscan Mission fathers sent deputies to the larger channel island of Santa Cruz and then advised the Viceroy in Mexico that the inhabitants of the Channel Islands should not be taken to the mainland missions. Conversion could eventually be accomplished by priests sent to the islands or even by setting up a mission on one. Spanish administrators wanted to avoid depopulation. At that time between 100 and 200 people may have lived on San Miguel.[2] This may be high; but there were certainly over 50, and migration from Santa Barbara was also a possibility.

The eighteenth century San Miguel islanders shared the lifeways of their fellow Chumash on the mainland, carried on a brisk trade with the some 200 villagers of Shisholop which lay twenty-six miles distant on the mainland and close to Point Conception, and as one would expect, intermarried and carried on other social exchanges. Like other islanders, they spoke a distinct dialect of the Chumash language; still they could attend the inter-island annual gatherings on Santa Cruz and carry out religious ceremonies in common with Chumash living elsewhere and apparently be understood. Thanks to these commonalties, the descriptions of Chumash mainlanders can be drawn upon in trying to reconstruct life on San Miguel at the time of European contact.

The Journals

The first Spanish parties to spearhead settlement of Upper California had a singular opportunity to observe and record all aspects of the Chumash culture. In spite of a religiosity unparalled in western Europe and a fierce pride in all things Spanish that drove them to destroy many aspects of the heathen cultures they encountered, their chroniclers wrote about what they saw. For example, Fray Juan Crespi and the engineer, Miguel Costanso, both kept journals as they accompanied Captain Portola on his 1769 and 1770 land marches between San Diego and Monterey. Juan Bautista Anza's party traveling in 1776 also had diarists. Perhaps the most poignant account comes from Jose Longinos Martinez, who under the sponsorship of the Spanish government was commissioned to study the plant life of the Spanish New World in 1792. Longinos Martinez reported to an enlightened and scientific group surrounding Charles III. His report fed into a comprehensive plan meant to update the scientific life of Spain and to catalog just what the colony in the New World had in the way of natural resources. Martinez readily conceded that the Santa Barbara Channel natives were far in advance of peoples either to the north or south of them and documented his findings.

Juan Bauitista Anza estimated that there were about 30 towns between today's Ventura and Point Conception with a total population of between 10 to 20 thousand. From Suisun Bay south he encountered non-agricultural peoples. But the Chumash impressed him in that they lived, in addition to gathering acorns, seeds, and fruits, by the bounty of the sea. They were also the most populous. At least one village numbered up to a thousand. In 1769 some islanders happened to be at the town named Shisholop when Crespi arrived, and they told Portola's party that twelve canoes had just gone out to the islands to bring in people who wanted to see the strangers. In 1770 when the party returned, the village was almost empty. The old men and women who remained told them that the villagers had all gone to Santa Cruz Island with their canoes. As Crespi sailed near Point Conception he saw San Miguel Island and saw sea lions on Richardson Rock which lay off its western extremity.

Every Spanish writer marveled at the Chumashs' canoe construction and his skill in handling it. The Portola party saw the Chumash ship yards south of Santa Barbara and called the town La Carpinteria. Here men worked the planks into shape, drilled holes for thongs to thread through and tie them together, and then sealed their work with asphaltum. Wrote Anza:

> *They have surprising skill and ability in construction of their canoes, which are made of good pine planks, well joined and of a graceful shape, with two prows. They handle them with equal skill; three or four men go out into the sea in them to fish, and they hold as many as ten men. They use long oars without bands, and row with indescribable lightness and speed.*[3]

Channel Islands National Park

A replica of the Indian canoe, the tomol.

Crespi observed that every town had canoes, counted 15 in one town, marveled at the keels and handsome work, and at their lightness which made it possible for only two of the "heathen" to launch a boat. Prior to the development of the plank canoe, travel between the islands and mainland was by means of tule balsas. The earliest evidence of plank canoe use by the Chumash dates from about 1300 years before the present. Archaeologists found rare pieces of planks with asphalt caulking and chert drills used to make the three holes for tying the planks together.[4]

The Spanish praised the Chumash for their craftsmanship and ability to work wood, stone, and shells without the use of iron and steel. Using chert knives they cut meat, opened fish, and carved wood. They were wide awake and well informed, and so inclined to commerce that Lt. Pedro Font called them the Chinese of California. The Chumash also traded with tribes who came from the interior. While adjectives such as gentle, peaceable, and generous filled their diaries, the Spanish also reported upon a warlike people who were almost incessantly fighting among themselves, village against village, often over boundary disputes. Longinos Martinez noted that even though the Indians were warlike, and proud, the fact that they lived in a fixed home made them obedient and responsible to their political and religious leaders.

Inside their spacious and well ventilated houses he saw beds made on the floor with skins and covers, noting that the otter pelt was highly prized in the Chumash culture and used to manufacture clothing, bed covers, and arrow quivers. Divisions separated the families as with cabins of a ship, and a fireplace at the center served for cooking. A well stocked storage house was attached to the side of the larger round dwelling. Men and women alike used the sweat house following it with a dive into cold water, and the mission fathers found the Chumash were fond of soaping and bathing themselves at all hours. Martinez, for all of his scientific objectivity, called this an addiction and the sweat bath a bad practice leading to a lack of robustness. He praised the dress, ornaments, and hair arrangement of the women, their skill in basketry, and conceived that the people's manner of painting themselves was done in order that they could know from which village each one came. Thus, when they met at a dance or inter-island function they could identify each person with a specific place. The San Miguelenos used a checkerboard facial paint design.

A stockade enclosed the "heathen" cemeteries, and some graves had painted board markers to indicate the occupation of the deceased. These did not offend the Spanish, but practices of public idolatry and multiple deities signaled a need for immediate conversion. Martinez wrote that the men had only one wife, one acquired with a simple contract by saying "You love me and I love you." Marriage was followed by what the Spanish viewed as the unchristian and barbarous practice of causing abortion of the first pregnancy under the belief that if that baby lived, the mother would never be pregnant again. Healthy babies were strapped to a small ladder, wrapped with grasses and bits of fur until they resembled a small bundle, and thereafter the baby was not carried. Mothers dragged the ladder from one place to another, and the baby lived in almost total inaction until it was old enough to walk. The Spanish foresaw a utopia in which their own values would be imposed, would replace the Chumash ways, and be practiced by all members of society.

Missions

The Spanish assigned the Franciscan Order the task of reordering Indian society, and to do this the Order established missions along the Santa Barbara Channel. These were places where the native peoples would be brought together or "reduced," converted to Catholicism, and made Spanish in every possible way. Military garrisons or presidios secured the missions and their inmates. In 1782 a garrison was in place, then funding came along for the Mission San Buenaventura. The missions at Santa Barbara (1786), La Purisima (1788), and Santa Inez (1804) followed. The land in between them was to be used for Spanish ranching and agriculture. Indian labor completed the concept of a mission-oriented great hacienda. Born of the Iberian reconquest when Spain fought for 700 years to drive the "heathen" Moors from the Peninsula and where the Spanish Catholic Church was assigned vast lands, the strategy of a Church's hacienda worked by flocks of neophytes fit California well. It contributed to the demise of the Chumash village, religion, political, trade, and social systems. In 1804 when the last of the mainlanders had fallen under the system there were still large groups of Chumash left on the islands. Fr. Estevan Tapis, President of the California Missions, suggested to the governor that he place a mission on Santa Cruz Island where there were many very poor and good-natured Chumash who would turn Christian with great pleasure. A measles epidemic on the islands and the questions of sufficient water, good soil, and money delayed a decision.

About this time foreigners hunting the otter brought along northwestern Indians to do the actual hunting for them and dropped them off on the Channel Islands. Clashes with the Chumash followed, and since the hunters were armed with modern weapons, they slaughtered many Indians. In 1811 the Kodiak Indians killed many of the villagers on San Nicholas Island. The fate of those on San Miguel is unknown, but the island once harbored many otters and could have been attractive to hunters. The Church hurriedly sent for the islanders bringing each group to the closest mainland mission between 1814 and 1816. For the San Miguelenos this meant La Purisima near present day Lompoc.

La Purisima Mission records reveal that the two towns on San Miguel Island were named Toan and Niuoiomi, the latter believed to be very small, perhaps one family. A total of 34 were baptized from Toan, three from Niuoiomi. An old La Purisima Indian is our sole source for all we know of the removal of the Chumash from San Miguel. He told others, and in particular Fernando Librado, one of the informants of ethnographer John P. Harrington, the following things:

> *In 1815 a priest at the La Purisima Mission ordered Captain Francisco Kuliwit to go to San Miguel Island with thirty canoes and bring back all of the Indians still there. Many Indians, according to this informant, had been taken off the island in about 1812, and twenty-four islanders, all sailors, had visited the island in 1815. The Wot, or captain, set out from Cojo Ranch with thirty canoes, but upon arriving at the sea they saw a great storm. Taking charge the Captain ordered his men to push him off into the water; however, he sent the others to Cojo Viejo, close to Gaviota, where it was calmer. Even there all but six canoes sank, and the Captain ordered them back. The Captain and his partner made it to the island. After this incredible tale of disaster, the informant added that a year later the last of the San Miguel Indians were brought to the mainland, thirty in all.*[5]

Mission archives do not hold any information upon the exodus, and even their baptismal records correlate poorly with this account of it. In any event, such an exodus apparently ended close to eleven thousand years of continuous occupancy of San Miguel Island.

How the San Miguelenos fared at Mission La Purisima will probably never be known. We are reasonably sure that none ever returned to the island, and that instead these skilled fishermen and craftsmen and their heirs were destined for the lowest levels of the Hispanic class system. The revolt at La Purisima in 1824 causes us to wonder if, as neophyte cowboys and brick layers, they suffered more floggings than they were willing to endure. Ethnographer John Johnson identified in the mission records a man who was a chief from San Miguel and followed this chief and his lineage down to 1928. His descendants are no doubt alive today somewhere in Santa Barbara County. We are not discussing ancient man here. San Miguel Island supported this thriving population but a short time ago. Abraham Lincoln was a boy.

Chapter V

PINNIPEDS, SEA OTTERS, AND THE TRAPPERS

For thousands of years marine mammals hauled out onto the shores along the California coast and on the coastwise islands to rest and to breed unmolested. Sea otters lived along the shores beyond the breakers, and migrating whales crowded into such spots as Monterey Bay.[1] Although we lack specific knowledge about the ancient marine mammal population on San Miguel, the numbers could have been even greater than those we find there today.

Five species of pinnipeds (fin-footed marine mammals) now gather at San Miguel on a regular basis, and solitary representatives of a sixth species are occasionally spotted. This is the greatest variety to be found in any one place in the entire world. It is in good part explained by the fact that the island lies on an interface between two climatic conditions, one belonging to the Arctic northwest and the other to the Mexican coast. Prevailing weather and ocean currents allow the island to support marine life migrating from both extremes. The pinnipeds are found on the west end of San Miguel Island because this is where there are the best beaches and dependable fog cover. Elephant seals especially need the cooling effect of the fog. This is probably why there are only a few seen now and then on the beaches of Santa Rosa Island.

The Guadalupe fur seal reaches the northerly limits of its range on San Miguel while the northern fur seal and the Steller sea lion reach the southern limit of their habitats. The harbor seal, California sea lion, and the northern elephant seal complete the list of island residents. Point Bennett at the island's extreme west end is the most important pinniped rookery (breeding ground) on the island and in fact in California waters. Prehistoric islanders left the remains of all these mammals in garbage middens above the Point thus documenting their participation in the long food chain grounded in the ocean's upwelling off Point Conception and San Miguel Island.

With the exception of prehistoric hunting discussed above, close to primeval conditions for marine mammals ended on San Miguel when Anglo-American, Russian, and other foreigners traveled from the Aleutian Islands and along the coast of North America to hunt for marine mammals. They began to poach in Spanish California waters between 1796 and 1805.[2] The sea otter's luxurious pelt attracted the first wave of hunters, and the slaughter at San Miguel continued until the last otter was taken.

Hunting the Sea Otter

The northern habitats of the silky furred otter, the *Enhyrda lutris*, on the Pribilof and Aleutian Islands, were inadvertently located and opened to world exploitation by the Dane, Vitus Bering. Peter the Great sent Bering out in 1733 to reconnoiter and to search for an imaginary place called Gamaland. After eight years Bering reached the Gulf of Alaska where, suffering from scurvy and the cold, he died in 1741. His surviving crew members dined on the sea otter, wore its furs, and returned home. The Russians then introduced the otter fur to the rich market of Canton, China.[3] Fabulous prices propelled the hunters to travel the entire length of the otter habitat. It extended from the northerly Kurile Islands off Japan to the Kamchatka Peninsula, easterly along the Aleutian Islands and the Gulf of Alaska, and south along the continental coast and Channel Islands to Baja California. The otter's fur, developed to withstand the ocean's cold, was so dense and soft that only the coarse, outer layer got wet. The pelt gave off a shimmering gloss when it was shaken to expose lustrous white roots displayed against darkening brown or black fur tips. When pressed, it could stretch to five feet by two and a half feet. Sea otters lacked the blubber common to other marine mammals but their fur with its entrapped air insulated them. They also kept themselves warm by eating fifteen to thirty-eight percent, or on average a quarter of their body weight, daily. They pried mussels and abalone off rocks, cracked clam shells upon a stone they balanced upon their breasts, and dived for the sea urchin.[4]

Female otters usually give birth and nurse their young at sea, although some instances of land births have been observed. San Miguel kelp beds were an ideal nursery, a place where the mother could get under the kelp and in effect drape it around her body while she fed her pup. One observer described the otter as curious and playful and "seen to toss a piece of seaweed up in the air from paw to paw, apparently taking great delight in catching it before it could fall into the water."[5] Because of these human-like qualities much has been written about the otter, about cruel and crafty hunting techniques used to trap mother and pup, and also about the adventurous men who fought over them.

The Russian hunters found otters concentrated in the far north Pacific, scarce off Oregon and Washington, but abundant off California.[6] The Aleut Indians (also referred to as Kodiaks, for one of the islands on which they lived) had already mastered otter hunting. According to archaeological evidence they had killed so many that they disrupted the whole kelp bed ecosystem from which the otter fed. Taking advantage of their expertise, the Russians sent them out in their sleek skin-covered boats the Russians called *bidarkas* and arranged contracts with the Aleuts to harpoon set numbers of otters.[7] As the northern otters became scarce, a Boston merchant, Joseph O'Cain, proposed a commercial arrangement beneficial to Russians and Americans. He met with Governor Alexander Baranov, director of the Russian American Company, on Kodiak Island in 1803, and there they agreed that Baranov would supply the Aleuts and the *bidarkas* while O'Cain would provide transportation for them on his vessel the *O'Cain* to the new fields off California.[8]

The Spanish had already attempted to hunt otters in the Santa Barbara Channel and to export the skins. The

Ventura and Santa Barbara Mission fathers paid local Indians to hunt, but with little success as the Chumash lacked skills. They did not need warm clothing and killed only an occasional otter.[9] The Spanish set up regulations to keep out poachers and laws against killing otter pups, but the administration could not provide the patrol boats or the men to enforce the regulations. Foreigners hunted at will. The Bostonians confounded the Spanish by leaving a hundred or so northwest Indians (Aleuts) on the various islands and kept the transport ship near the mainland. This was a situation the Spanish could not cope with, and it was even more devastating for the island Indians because the armed Aleuts brutally attacked them.[10] Whether Aleuts were left on San Miguel Island, we do not know.

From the Alaskan waters the ships would come directly to California without doing any hunting along the way. The Aleut hunters brought along their *bidarkas* and their women and harvested 3,000 to 5,000 pelts a trip out. Ship owners issued guns and buckshot to the northwest Indians, thus arming them for the hunt and for fighting off competition. Setting out with several canoes, they would surround the otter, wait out his dives till he was exhausted, and usually harpoon the catch. One 1807 account read, "The *O'Cain* had now from seventy to eighty canoes, carrying about a hundred and fifty Kodiak Indian hunters, fitted out and hunting sea otter among the islands." So dependent were the foreigners upon northwest Indians that Captain Winship of the *O'Cain* complained in 1810 that he could not work around the Santa Barbara Islands unless he had Aleut hunters.[11]

The next year he came properly equipped and took away 3,952 pelts to sell in Canton, China. Pelt counts were often broken down into adults, yearlings, and pups thus documenting the thorough and indiscriminate nature of the killings.

In 1812 the Russians built Fort Ross north of San Francisco using it not only as a provisioning base for the otter hunt but also as a staging area to bring in the fur seal and the sea lion. The foreigners and the Aleuts eventually came into conflict with some of our American Mountain Men who had chased the river otter out west and then turned to hunting the sea otter. Yankee frontiersmen entered California by land in the late 1820's, and a team of California historians wrote of them:

> *...these tough, durable, resourceful men came out of the east and broached the bulwark that nature and the Spanish erected around Alta California.... Tempered in the waters of a thousand icy streams, steeled by conflict with Indians, made resourceful by years of grappling with a demanding and hostile environment, the mountain men received an uncertain welcome when they came wandering out of the desert country of Southern California. The resident population had good reason to look with reserve on these sun-blackened, leather-clad, grease-laden representatives of an alien land and culture....they were a reckless breed—an American original as hard as the hardest thing that could happen to [them].*[12]

The Mountain Men took on the Aleuts with ease. George Nidever, who had a sheep ranch on San Miguel Island for eighteen years, proved this when he hunted otters around the islands. Seeking a warmer climate, he had joined the Walker expedition and was in the first American party to make an east-west crossing of the Sierras in June, 1834. Once in California he hunted around San Francisco Bay where he learned that while a river otter's pelt brought $2, a sea otter's fur brought $30. Sailing for Santa Barbara, he teamed up with Daniel Sills in 1835 and went to sea.[13] Like other Rocky Mountain fur trappers who came to Santa Barbara, Nidever hunted under Goodwin Dana's license. Dana led the way when he arrived in 1826, became a Mexican citizen, and then Captain of the Port.[14]

Isaac Galbraith preceded Nidever in the hunt around San Miguel and the other islands. He had staggered into the Mission San Gabriel after a sixty-day walk from Utah in 1826 and was the first of the "reckless breed" to switch from trapping river beavers to chasing sea otters.

Galbraith's method, used by Nidever as well, was to shoot at the otters, then direct hired Kanakas (Hawaiians) to swim out and bring in the game. Gradually California Indians were trained and used until they superseded the Kanakas.[15]

If not the first, George Nidever was the most outstanding hunter of this whole period and surely the most celebrated historical figure ever associated with the island. Prior to his trip to California he had spent thirteen years trapping, fighting Indians, and building a reputation as one of the best shots in the west. Fellow hunters bet up to $5,000 on him to kill more buffalo than any other man in the Rocky Mountains. As for Indians, he remembered one attack of four or five hundred Indians on the Walker party this way:

> *"....Thirty-four of the Indians advanced in a body, and 15 of our men, myself among the number, were ordered out to meet them. From 50 to 60 yards from our company, we halted and awaited the Indians. We allowed them to get quite close before opening fire, but when we did shoot it was with such telling effect that but one of the 34 escaped."*[16]

His fame spread even further when he shot forty-five grizzly bears in one year.

In 1836 Nidever, Burton Sparks, and a black hunter named Allen Light, but whom they quickly renamed Black Steward, headquartered on Santa Rosa Island to the immediate east of San Miguel along with five Kanakas and other hunters. The party knew that the Aleuts often claimed the islands for their own headquarters and that they were armed and unpredictable. The Aleuts had exterminated whole villages of the native Indians, killed livestock, and had at one time set upon Sparks and Steward and captured their supplies. Nidever told of a morning in 1836 when some of the Aleuts paddled toward the island in the fog and almost cut himself, Sparks, and Steward who were fishing from canoes, off from the shore.

Nidever's sharpshooting saved them as he helped kill at least three Aleuts and wound several others. The next day when Nidever and his party were on shore, through the lifting fog they sighted a brig two or three miles off shore unloading eleven canoes. The Indians paddled toward the shore and stopped to fish in the kelp, but suddenly all of them headed for shore. Again the mountain men's marksmanship was superior to that of the northwest Indians and they returned to the brig which sailed away the following day. Nidever claimed this was the first reversal the Indians had suffered in the area and went on to describe their history of cruelties around the islands.[17]

In Nidever's account the brig from which the Indians operated was captained by John Bancroft, and the next year Bancroft anchored off San Miguel Island in command of a different ship, the *Lama*. Apparently, there was trouble from several sources: Bancroft drank excessively, his Kanaka wife let the 25 Indian hunters aboard know that she felt them racially inferior, and Bancroft cut down on the food to punish the hunters when the hunt went poorly. On November 16, 1836, two of the canoes came back with only three otter skins; on the 20th two more canoes returned from Santa Cruz Island with only eight. On the 23rd when all the canoes returned there were bad words. The Indians armed themselves, shot Bancroft, and seriously wounded his wife.[18]

Bancroft had been poaching in Mexican waters, and it was men like him who convinced the governor of Alta California that he should urge Mexican citizens to petition for land grants out on the Channel Islands. Ranchers should settle there and protect the surrounding waters. While Santa Cruz and Santa Rosa Islands became land grants, there were no petitioners for San Miguel.

During the 1830's the hunt changed. New regulations forced the Russians to work under Mexican law and to split the proceeds with the Mexican government. Two-thirds of the hunters the Russians used had to be California Indians. Also, by this time the Indian gangs were no longer limited to lassos, harpoons, spears, and buckshot. The ship captains gave them guns. Rifles and English muskets stepped up the slaughter. Nidever told an interviewer, "The range of these guns is something incredible. Our men assured us that the bullets from the Indians' guns passed them when they were fully a mile from the beach."[19] Legal restrictions, patrol boats, decreasing returns, and the gradual extinction of the sea otter forced the Russian American Company to withdraw and to close down Fort Ross in 1841.

The greatest otter harvest had been in the 1820's and mountaineer George Yount wrote that even in the 1830's he saw them lying near land at the islands in groups of several hundreds.[20] Only a few men could support themselves from pelts in 1870, and when Nidever died in 1883 the otters were all but gone. Some otters were killed near San Miguel Island in 1890 when, due to scarcity, the price was up to $475 on the London Market.[21] The last individual otter on the California coast was reportedly killed in 1911 off the Monterey Peninsula.[22]

Pinniped Haulouts, Rookeries, and Knockdowns

Tracing the evolution of the present-day North Pacific Ocean pinnipeds through the fossil record, paleontologists have found some evidence of ancestors 23 million years old. The true seals appeared about a million and a half years before the present. Thus it is possible that San Miguel's marine mammals hauled out on her beaches in the early Pleistocene even though we have no faunal evidence that old on the island. Pinnipeds are sea mammals which live on both land and sea. These ancient seals, sea lions, and elephant seals lumbered onto shore to rest in the sun, molt, give birth to their young, and breed. Marine biologists identify a rookery as an area where pups are born and use the term haulout when the site is only used for resting. San Miguel's broad sandy beaches and rocky slopes were ideal for both. In addition, the island had no predators such as wolves, coyotes, or grizzly bears.

Many mammalogists believe that pinnipeds never used the California mainland beaches to any great extent because of grizzly bear predation. Yet, in the island waters there were marine predators such as the killer whale and the sharks. As the pinniped population increased, those predators could increase in population accordingly.[23]

Of the six pinniped species on San Miguel Island today the breeding species include the California sea lion *Zalophus californianus,* the Steller sea lion *Eumetopias jubatus,* the northern fur seal *Callorhinus ursinus,* the harbor seal *Phoca vitulina,* and the northern elephant seal *Mirounga angustirostris.* The Guadalupe fur seal *Arctocephalus townsendi* currently makes this island the northerly limit of its range using the island as a haulout site.

Dana Seagars

Sea elephants and sea lions at Point Bennett.

The sea lions and fur seals derive from ancestors that appeared 22 to 23 million years ago, ancestors that belonged to the same family as the modern bear. Since they are not totally pelagic (oceanic) or terrestrial, they must have had to make certain adaptations for both environments. For example, to maintain a constant body temperature the fur seals came to depend largely upon a coat of short stiff hairs over a heavy underfur so fine that water never touched the skin. Other pinnipeds developed a layer of blubber beneath their thick skin. The fur seal male is known to weigh up to 600 pounds, but the blubber-protected northern sea lion male averages 2,000 pounds. Adaptation for dives that could last up to an hour has been met by reserving dissolved oxygen in the blood and muscle tissue for the brain and heart. The heart beat slows to 20 to 25 percent of its normal surface rate, digestion slows, and muscles operate on a supply of oxygen stored in their tissues.[24]

Breeding and nursing for all of these pinnipeds occur along shorelines or on ice packs. The mother gives birth, leaves her pup on shore with other pups, feeds at sea, and returns to nurse her young on rich milk. She may conceive a new baby within several days to a month after having given birth. However, nature provides for delayed implantation of the newly fertilized ovum in order to accommodate for several factors. First, the mother must nurse her pup which is still unable to go to sea. Secondly, the gestation period (development of the new embryo) can take up to eleven months. Finally, she must be given time to return to the same rookery to give birth a year later. The delayed implantation is so finely-tuned that the mother indeed will return to the rookery to give birth just one year from the time she had previously arrived.[25]

The first threat to the pinniped's supremacy on the islands probably came about 10,000 years ago with the first arrival of man. These predators being small in number and using rock tools took comparatively few of the animals using the meat for food, hides for clothing and shelter, and bones for tools and supportive devices. A study of the fur seals along California's coasts revealed that the Indian garbage middens on San Miguel had more bones of fur seals in them than of any other pinniped.[26] We know also that by the nineteenth century the Chumash economy at San Miguel was heavily dependent upon trade and that the

Indians butchered sea mammals for prime portable cuts to sell on the mainland. The San Miguelenos impact upon the pinniped and otter populations was discussed earlier in Chapter 4.

Fur Seals

Massive harvests of the fur seal reached a peak in the South Pacific during the eighteenth century. As the valuable sea otter was exterminated in the North Pacific and in the Bering Sea, a Russian fur company sent out Gerassim Pribilof in 1786 to search for an island where fur seals went ashore. After three years on the foggy sea, Pribilof discovered the Bering Sea islands which now bear his name. They were covered with fur seals. By taking up to 200,000 a year the Russians harvested about two and a half million pelts before they sold Alaska to the United States. As the Pribilof herds dwindled, the hunt again proceeded southward. Off Southern California hunters may have found both the northern fur seal and the Guadalupe fur seal. In tallying their kill, hunters did not distinguish between the two species, so we do not know for certain what species were taken. Fur seals were the most desirable kill of all the pinnipeds, and the hunt ranged world-wide. When it reached San Miguel is not known, but in 1800 the island was considered an important source. Harvests in California peaked in about 1835.[27] Although the fur was the most valuable product, the flesh of the young was said to taste like mutton and the hearts and livers of the young were considered a delicacy.

Charles Melville Scammon sailed out of San Francisco on sealing hunts between 1852 and 1873. His account of what he saw on his voyages between Baja California and the Pribilof Islands is our first narrative describing the fur seal rookeries of the Channel Islands. The material below is from his chapter about fur seals along the California coast, and there is some question as to whether Scammon saw fur seals or sea lions. He stated that from a distance it was difficult to distinguish between a fur seal and a sea lion.

Despite the confusion his observations are valuable. He recalled that in the early years when the fur seals were abundant, they were easily killed with an ordinary seal club. The crew, some twenty men, would get between the seals and the water, raise a lot of noise, and then slay the animals right and left by one or two blows on the head. Hundreds were taken in these "knock downs." When the animals became scarce, the boat would leave a few men on the island to watch out for single mammals approaching the island and then shoot them one at a time as they came ashore. He wrote of gullies fronting on California beaches, gullies such as we find on San Miguel, and of how the men drove the animals as far back up into the land as they could so that none of them could get away. Since only the two- and three-year olds yielded prime skins, the flock was screened as they drove them inland so that the older seals could escape. Another reason for driving them inland was to get them away from the breeding ground since the blood and carcasses disturbed the other animals.[28] By 1850 the fur seal was almost extinct. The last recorded fur seal catch in California was on Richardson Rock, about seven miles northwest of San Miguel Island and almost inaccessible to man. Hunters took five seals off the Rock in 1890.[29]

Northern Elephant Seals

For centuries the whale had supplied meat to Europeans and in the seventeenth century was known best as the world's prime source of oil for lighting and soap making.[30] In the summer, when the gray whales were gone and after 1800 when they were generally depleted, whalers went after the northern elephant seal. An elephant seal bull eighteen feet long can yield 210 gallons of oil. Some specimens that grow to be twenty-two feet long and weigh 5,000 pounds produce more. The northern elephant seal population has grown considerably in recent years. These are now the most abundant pinniped on San Miguel Island.[31]

Although slow and lumbering, elephant seals have been found sunning themselves on island cliffs fifty to sixty feet above the sea. These seals follow an uncertain ocean migration route for much of the year, but from January through April they seek out the breeding rookeries. Harems consist of a male and eight to forty females. Even the bachelor elephant seal comes on shore, stays until it is fully shed, and loses up to half of its fat. They rest in the sun using their flippers to throw sand on raw patches of skin, to keep cool, and to keep off flies. Hunters captured them in knock downs. Occasionally, a large male would give battle, but one well-placed musket ball, a lance through the roof of the mouth, or a clubbing by two men with heavy oaken clubs beating at its head would kill it. In their panic, elephant seals smothered each other. After the kill, the men would flay the skin with a large knife for the whole length and cut out pieces of fat about eight by fifteen inches. These were hauled out to the boat by ropes and there boiled in pots to extract the oil.[32] The elephant seal had a close brush with extinction, and in 1892, the known population was reduced to nine on Guadalupe Island, none on San Miguel.

Sea Lions

The California and the northern (Steller) sea lions which were hunted on San Miguel Island supplied several products useful to man: a silky skin for luxury items, oil, the sex organs of bulls that were sold to the Chinese as a cure for impotence, and the whiskers. The last were used as ornaments and to clean opium pipes. Many animals were taken simply to satisfy the "trimmings" trade in genitalia and whiskers. For this the genitalia were dried, powdered, and shipped to China.

The sea lion was fearful of man, and to escape would roll, tumble and sometimes make leaps from high rocks to get away. As in the hunts of other sea mammals, they were clubbed; but they fled rapidly, and not many would be around if the crew did only this. Charles M. Scammon, in describing the sea lion rookeries on the Channel Islands wrote that the adult males were shot in the ear or near it. A

Mike Maki

California Sea Lion male, his harem and pups at Point Bennett.

shot in any other part of the body had little effect. He saw sea lions on every beach, rock and cliff at Santa Barbara Island. The animals became so familiar with the ways of the hunters that when they saw the boats lowered in the morning, they would swim out to sea only to return when they saw the shore boats leaving the island.[33] As the elephant seals became scarce in the 1860's, sea lions and seals were sought for their oil and the herds severely depleted by 1870. California hunters captured seals at San Miguel both for oil and to sell them for exhibition. A man was observed on San Miguel Island with a large kettle set where he rendered the sea lion blubber for its oil. He was selling a barrel of oil for fifty cents, the skin for five to seven cents a pound, and the sex organs to the Chinese.[34]

Making it Back to a Protected Island

When Benjamin Silliman, a geologist, claimed in the 1860's that California had more oil in its soil than all the whales in the Pacific Ocean, he was correctly predicting the end of the sea mammal oil industry.[35] By 1900 whale and seal hunting could no longer compete with the expanding oil industry and the great slaughter was over. One by one pinniped survivors made their way back to ancient habitats such as San Miguel Island to proliferate on the isolated beaches. But even as the new colonies attempted to reestablish themselves, a new breed of hunters came to harvest the seals and sea lions for their trimmings, for pet food manufacturers, and for public display. Their clumsy methods caused the deaths of hundreds of sea lions in the late 1920's and 1930's. However, despite this mortality commercial fishermen complained to the California Department of Fish and Game that proliferating sea lions were eating their fish. Fish and Game sent out a biologist, Paul Bonnot, to make a count in 1927, the first systematic survey of sea lion rookeries on San Miguel Island. Bonnot photographed and mapped the rookeries and haulout areas, documenting that the northern or Steller sea lion bred on Richardson, Castle, and other San Miguel offshore rocks. The California sea lion bred primarily on Castle Rock. He also witnessed the aftermath of one hunt and wrote:

> *"A large number of sea lions were killed at San Miguel Island... The beach at Flea [Castle] Island contained a mixed rookery of nearly 400 sea lions when I visited it on June 13 [1927]. Two days later I again landed there. In the meantime the sea lion hunter had done his work. Every pup on the rookery was dead and of the 400 animals which I counted on my first visit, a pitiful remnant of 30 or 40 was swimming timidly about in the surf."*[36]

In the 1940's the fishing industry wanted a bill passed to promote hunting; instead, a bill was passed to afford sea lions protection. This did not put a stop to illegal "sport" hunting, a Sunday boat ride out to the islands to shoot at the seals as they lay motionless on the rocks. San Miguel suffered less than the more accessible islands. There was, however, random killing of sea lions for another decade.[37] The Steller sea lions increased until 1938 and then began a decline in pupping and in haulouts which continues today. Carefully-watched San Miguel was for some time the only breeding place for the Stellar sea lion in Southern California; however, no pupping was observed there in the 1985-1987 seasons.[38]

Census counts of San Miguel Island's six pinnipeds demonstrate the wide variation in the size of colonies. Outstripping them all is the elephant seal, and its return can be traced to 1938 when observers counted thirteen on the island. Mammalogists relate this migration to a law passed in 1911 in Mexico when that government prohibited the elephant seal kill in its waters. Following this the population on Guadalupe Island off Baja California recovered to form a nucleus. From this, individuals probably migrated back to San Miguel. In 1965 the California Department of Fish and Game commenced an annual census, and wardens estimated that there were about 3,000 on San Miguel sighting most of the elephant seals at Point Bennett and along the southern shore of the island where wide expanses of sand predominate.[39] During the breeding season, January and February, the elephant seal population reaches its peak, and in 1981 6,800 seals were counted on the island: about 4,300 were on Point Bennett and the rest elsewhere. In 1987 10,120 pups were born translating into an estimated population of 35,420.[40]

The California sea lion herd has grown steadily at the island, from 1,117 in 1951 to an estimated population of 4,715 in 1986. These have been seen chiefly in rookeries at Point Bennett and to its southeast at Tyler Bight.[41] The northern or Steller sea lion traditionally used San Miguel Island and its associated islets (Castle, Wilson, and Richardson Rocks) for hauling sites, and it too returned. Throughout the Southern California Bight (see Introduction) the number of breeding Steller sea lions has persistently declined over the past fifty years. Mammalogists observe a competition between the California sea lion and the Steller sea lion for such sites as Richardson Rock which helps account for the very low numbers of the Steller seal found there today. In fact the last Stellar reported on San Miguel Island was in 1984,a large male trying to mate with a California Fur Seal.[42]

Harbor seals now pup on San Miguel at several small coves and sandy beaches such as Otter Harbor (which lies along the east side of Harris Point), and breeding probably takes place in the nearshore waters adjacent to these locales. Aerial surveys conducted by the Southwest Fisheries Center in La Jolla recorded a high of 1,150 harbor seals in 1987, down to 928 in 1989.[43]

The return of both the Guadalupe Fur seal and the northern fur seal were considered dramatic events since their major habitats lie long distances from San Miguel Island. A few Guadalupe fur seals were seen at Point Bennett in 1969 and have been seen each year since. However, they breed only on Guadalupe Island. Investigations in the 1970's showed that this was the only member of the genus *Arctocephalus* to reside in the northern hemisphere, and it was listed as a threatened species under the Endangered Species Act in 1985.[44]

Channel Islands National Park

Guadelupe Fur Seals who make the island the northerly limit of their range.

The northern fur seal, it would seem, would stay in the Bering Sea where it thrived on polar temperatures. Marine specialists argued about whether this northern seal had in the past ever inhabited California waters. Perhaps all of the fur seals taken in the early nineteenth century were the Guadalupe fur seal. On July 21, 1968 biologists on a Smithsonian biological expedition tumbled through the surf in a rubber boat toward Adams Cove southeast of Point Bennett on a census mission. To their amazement they almost tripped over a breeding colony of Northern fur seals lolling on the beach: about forty females and their pups. Four of the mothers wore tags showing that they had been born on the Pribilof Islands. Another had been tagged on the far off Commander Islands near the Kamchatka Peninsula. San Miguel had the first known rookery of northern fur seals south of the Bering Sea. Robert L. Delong, a Smithsonian biologist, quickly spread the news: San Miguel Island was the only island in the North Pacific with six species of pinnipeds.[45]

In 1915 the biologist H.C. Bryant reported that thirty-two sea otters were clustered near Point Sur. The presence of this relic population was not publicized till 1939 after highway workers along Route l in Big Sur spotted another raft of some forty otters. In 1955 a biologist claimed that he saw two otters at the western end of Cuyler Harbor, San Miguel Island; but when zoologists from UCLA flew over the island in a helicopter at 100 feet in 1958 they could not spot a single otter. Harbor seals are abundant in these waters, and they could have been mistaken for sea otters.[46] The California coastal sea otter range today extends from about Cape Ano Nuevo to Point Conception, and individual otters have been observed in Cojo Anchorage near Point Conception which is about twenty miles from San Miguel.

Theoretical calculations by marine biologists directed into the past reveal that the California population could have been as high as 16,000 to 18,000. Yet, in the spring of 1991 only 1,941 were actually counted. The otter is exceptionally vulnerable to oil spills because its fur, which serves as a trap for an insulating layer of air, can become matted with oil and thus ineffective. Cold ocean water can penetrate to the skin, and under these conditions the otter typically dies of hypothermia or else pneumonia. In 1987 the California Coastal Commission approved a plan to translocate the nucleus of a new breeding colony to San Nicholas Island, 61 miles from the mainland, where it might survive should the central California colony be eliminated by a disaster such as a massive oil spill. Federal scientists took 139 otters out to San Nicholas Island waters, but only fourteen remained in the spring of 1991. At least 33 had swum back to the coast. Nonetheless, the translocation experiment was continued.

In early May, 1991, the scientists discovered nine adults and a pup in the waters off the northwest end of San Miguel Island. These were generally supposed to be some of the missing animals from the San Nicholas group which had managed to swim the seventy mile distance between the islands. Ironically, U.S. Fish and Wildlife Service would be obligated to move these otters since the agency had an

Bill Roberts

Elephant Seals, an easy shot for Sunday hunters.

agreement with the Southern California shellfish industry to maintain San Miguel as an otter-free zone. This brings to mind the otter's propensity for consuming shellfish.[47]

While the end of the great hunts allowed sea mammals to live again on San Miguel, man's changing attitude toward the environment and toward treatment of animals has enhanced their chance to survive. We protect the returnees. Until this century our concern with the environment centered upon what the environment did to us. We intellectualized about how the American frontier positively shaped our character and praised buffalo shooters such as Nidever who set themselves off from the crowd, like Hemmingway figures, by killing hundreds of animals in a single day. We leveled forests and killed animals without knowing about interrelated food webs, ecosystems, or how the life of one species affected the lives of others. Nineteenth century gentlemen along the California coast shot at sea lions purely for diversion.[48] Week end boaters took guns out to San Miguel to shoot

Dana Seagars

Northern Elephant seal

Dana Seagars

Northern Fur Seal nursery on Castle Rock.

and for the fun of seeing targeted sea lions fall off the rocks right up until the island was afforded federal protection.[49]

During World War II coastal regulations kept small boats away from the island, but immediately after the war the sharpshooters were back. Further, the Navy used it as a bombing range with the expected disturbance to the rookeries. Luckily, most targets were off the east end of the island since that placement afforded the ideal practice run. The largest rookeries lay eight miles to the west. The Pacific Missile Range testing program used the island land mass, but did not explode missiles on the island. Naval exercises in the long run eliminated some of the island's most unwanted visitors. This was because the Navy had to enforce some control over the boaters since it could not afford to disrupt its exercise schedule while it cleared the waters of small boats. Troublesome boaters were still using the seals for target practice. The Navy signed an agreement with the Park Service relating to protection of natural values in 1963, and zoologists, the Sierra Club, and conservationists demanded an end to the tests. At this time the Navy could not give up its testing program at San Miguel, but overall it needed a protective zone to keep the boaters out. A danger zone to be recognized "during firing practice only" was established. Since practice was often, the rookeries enjoyed a peripheral benefit.

The Park Service trained and informed the Navy about rookery safeguards and disturbances. More protection followed when San Miguel's pinnipeds fell under the provisions of the 1972 Marine Mammal Protection Act. The National Marine Fisheries Service now monitors the pinnipeds on San Miguel for the Park Service. Specialists for each species assess population trends, put forth recommendations to protect breeding areas and foraging habitats, monitor disturbances such as oil platforms and leasing, and keep an eye on the gill nets used by coastal fishermen. At the same time the Park Service monitors visitor impact upon the breeding mammals, enforcing necessary regulations about access to Point Bennett.

Our changing attitudes are reflected in the laws we have passed and the public money we are willing to spend. Some laws offer greater protection for animals than for people. Where the National Park Service budgeted $605 in fiscal year 1942 for the protection and restoration of unique wild life on San Miguel and the two other islands it administers, in 1991 the figure for protection and administration of the five-island national park was closer to two million dollars.[50]

Chapter VI

UNITED STATES SOVEREIGNTY: SHIPWRECKS AND NAVIGATIONAL AIDS

During the periods of Spanish and Mexican rule (1769-1848) little effort was put into mapping the Channel Islands or into sounding the ocean depths surrounding them. San Miguel Island was never occupied in any legal way, although Raemundo Carrillo, claimant of Santa Rosa Island, did ask the Mexican governor for the island in 1845. He failed to follow up with a formal claim.[1] Thus, in 1848, with the signing of the Treaty of Guadeloupe Hidalgo, San Miguel Island was unsurveyed government land and came to the United States as public domain. In the Treaty none of the Channel Islands were specifically mentioned. However, Upper California was clearly marked off by a southern boundary which ran across the Colorado River following the division line between Upper and Lower California. Scattered pronouncements that the islands belonged to Mexico or were free and sovereign in themselves persisted for many years.

In 1964 three squatters filed a grant deed in Santa Barbara County and went to court claiming San Miguel Island. The United States District Court promptly ordered them off the island and proclaimed the grant deed null and void.[2]

Actually, a Geological Survey pamphlet now kept as title evidence by the U.S. Naval Real Estate Division effectively set the issue to rest at an early date.[3] It argued that the boundaries of California were described fully in the state constitution of 1849 and that San Miguel Island was among the islands listed both as part of the state and as a part of the territory ceded to the United States. Congress approved the California constitution on August 31, 1852 and appropriated funds for subdivision of the off-shore islands so that they could be disposed of under the laws of the United States. The United States Supreme

Court acted on a case relating to the land grant on the neighboring island of Santa Cruz in 1859, patents were issued for land on various islands by the General Land Office, and eventually reservations were made for lighthouses. No formal claim was ever presented by the Mexican government, and it is certain that none could be made now with any hope of reversing the matter.

The Americans, steeped in a long tradition of supplying their shipping interests with nautical charts and their pioneers with land surveys, dispatched mapping teams to the west coast even before California was granted statehood. Undoubtedly, the gold rush of 1849, the increased shipping it generated along the California coast, and reports of shipwrecks inspired Congress to allocate funds promptly. Unavoidable delays and indecision over where to place navigational aids followed. For close to a century ships in the dark were driven into the islands and rocks along the Santa Barbara Channel, and the potential for danger is still there.

The Coast Surveyors at Work

The United States Coast Survey had been working around the entire country beginning at the coast of Maine, and in the spring of 1850 it sent out a party to commence primary triangulations for the California islands. These surveyors were the first Americans to write down descriptions of San Miguel Island. At the onset, Survey Assistant George Davidson camped near Point Conception and sketched a map simply to locate the islands. Coast Survey habitually borrowed a detail of naval officers for hydrographical work, and the following year it put Navy Lieutenant Commander James Alden in charge of coastal reconnaissance so he could examine anchorages and depths from Monterey to San Diego. As he and his men progressed he sent his data to Alexander Dallas Bache, Superintendent of U.S. Coast Survey, 1843-1867. Alden sketched San Miguel's contours, provided tidal information, and discovered that San Miguel had reefs on the north and west. He called Cuyler Harbor by name, describing it as one and seven-eighths miles wide at the mouth with a good deep landing, a sandy beach, and without surf.[4]

He apparently named the harbor after his colleague Navy Lieutenant Richard M. Cuyler. Alden praised Cuyler in his correspondence with Bache writing in 1853, "I know of no one in the service who is better qualified for taking charge of a hydrographic party than Mr. Cuyler."[5] Accordingly, Bache placed Cuyler in charge of a hydrographic party in Puget Sound in 1855. In those days geographical points were often named after fellow members of survey parties.

In the spring of 1852 the U. S. Senate asked what it would cost to complete a land and shore survey of the islands in the vicinity of the Santa Barbara Channel and specified each by name calling San Miguel Island "San Bernardo" as it had been under the Spanish. Bache calculated the costs of maps, charts, and engravings and ordered a survey that should:

> *...connect these islands with each other, and with the mainland, should determine the latitudes and longitudes of prominent points, should give the topography of the surface of each, and the hydrography of the shores as far seaward as may be necessary and including a general examination of the vicinity.*[6]

Bache got $136,000 to cover ship rentals, salaries, food, and equipment, and it was not enough.

Captain Edward O.C. Ord and two assistants, George Davidson and W.E. Greenwell, came west to triangulate the islands in 1853. First, they would need to measure a series of triangles connecting the islands to each other and to known points on the mainland. Many of the sides would be common to adjacent mainland triangles, and the highly elevated angles or points were called stations and marked, usually with a braced pole.[7]

Meanwhile, the naval contingent under Alden was

making soundings from Point Conception to San Miguel Island, thence to San Nicholas Island, to San Clemente Island, and on to San Diego. Alden recommended a lighthouse for either Anacapa or Santa Cruz Island. Anacapa finally got one...48 years later.

In 1856, the job still incomplete, W. E. Greenwell took out a new party to make triangulations with orders from Bache to give the Channel Islands priority over the mainland due to the heavy shipping traffic. The base for main triangulation was the Los Angeles plan already in place, so Greenwell stationed himself at the San Pedro Hill Station and tried to throw points for a triangle reaching to Catalina and Santa Barbara Islands and Point Dume. Once these points were established, a line could reach out to Santa Cruz Island and teams could work on the islands farther west: Santa Rosa and San Miguel. Greenwell wrote that the plan involved "four long lines all centering on the little island of Santa Barbara....This little island was the turning point, as it were, or where these four long lines centered, the shortest of which would be 35 miles more or less."[8] After the main triangulation points were established, heliotropes, mirrored instruments which threw the sun's rays, would be posted.

As an easterner Greenwell had not anticipated the California coastal fogs, so he had an unexpected problem with visibility. During the two months he spent at San Pedro trying to observe Santa Barbara Island it was only visible for nine days. The winter brought little rain, the islands were enveloped in thick fog, while the mainland was fairly clear. Greenwell concentrated on the mainland and this irritated Bache. By April Greenwell was sick and wrote Bache that the dampness and wind on the west coast made east coast service seem like a mere exercise. In January his budget was cut from $12,000 to $7,198, so he worked another month, broke camp, and called it quits for the year.

San Miguel Island had no budget for 1857, but in May of 1858 funds were assigned and Greenwell set sail on the schooner *Humboldt* and began secondary triangulations there. He marked ten stations and described their surroundings. He never once described a tree, only cactus, sage, and dark looking bushes. West of "Green Mountain" Station he saw a huge strip of sand drift. During the summers of 1860 and 1861 survey parties tried to complete the secondary triangulations, but no topographic work was attempted. The Civil War ended the survey as money depreciated and Greenwell's men threatened to accept only gold for pay. When communication with Bache in Washington was cut off the team disbanded.

Throughout the job Bache failed to understand west coast weather. Unexpected sickness from exposure crippled his crews, and they wrote him that at Point Conception they took the heaviest gale they had ever seen. Their camp was just across the channel from San Miguel Island. Stehman Forney led a Coast Survey party out to San Miguel in 1871-1872. He sketched the topography and placed a bench mark on the southerly tip of tiny Prince Island in Cuyler Harbor. Then Forney drew more triangulations and erected signals (stations) at eleven new points. Looking down on the water from Harbor Station he saw a hill to the right covered with sand. Greenwell had seen the same hill in 1858 covered with low sage brush and cactus: thus, considerable stripping, erosion, and sand dune migration had taken place in the dozen years between. Forney's observation matched the recollections of the hunter and sheep rancher, George Nidever, who recalled the drought and the heavy grazing of the hungry sheep he ran there in the early 1860's.[9] Forney positioned Richardson Rock seven miles northwest of Point Bennett. With Forney's log books and recommendations in, the U.S. government was aware of the options for anchorage needs and navigational aids all along the Santa Barbara Channel.

Shipwrecks

Ever since Juan Cabrillo's voyage when he turned back short of Point Conception to take refuge on San Miguel Island, we have read of sea captains who sailed the Santa

Barbara Channel using the Islands for emergency anchorages. Some vessels sailing great distances and to save time, stayed far outside the island chain as did the Manila Galleons. Yet many of those heading for Panama during the Gold Rush era took the deep Channel which lay between the islands of Anacapa, Santa Cruz, Santa Rosa, and San Miguel and the Santa Barbara coast. Traveling south from San Francisco the ships rounded Point Conception, turned east, and entered the foggiest and roughest waters off the California coast. Conditions could worsen quickly when the prevailing northwest winds reached gale force or when there were sudden changes in visibility. It was at Point Conception that ships were committed to either bear northeastward and thread their way down the channel or to continue sailing south but far enough to the west to miss Richardson Rock and San Miguel Island. When gale force winds, high seas and zero visibility combined navigation got out of control. Ships could go aground at the Rock seven miles northwest of San Miguel Island, or on the west end of San Miguel Island at Point Bennett, or on the reefs at Simonton Cove, (north shore).

The number of ships that met their end on San Miguel Island has never been catalogued. Ships of United States registry, if wrecked, can be located in the *List of Merchant Vessels of the United States* which enters vessels by year and provides the home port. The Lighthouse Service throughout the years provided wreck reports based on that data. But in the last half of the nineteenth century when hundreds of lumber schooners were beating their way through the fog off California and occasionally colliding with a rock or an island, records of these wrecks rarely reached the east coast files. Local newspapers occasionally recorded small boat sinkings. However, divers and salvage crews probably know more about numbers of sunken ships than anyone. Peter Howorth of Santa Barbara has been such a diver, and is looked upon as the unofficial dean of channel shipwrecks and marine archaeology. He once claimed during a discussion about the perils of Point Arguello and Honda to the north that, "You'll probably see a lot more wreckage any day of the week on Point Bennett at the western tip of San Miguel. More ships have been wrecked there than on any other spot along the California coast."[10]

Divers report that there is evidence of a Spanish galleon sunk in 1801 lying off the west end of the island.[11] In 1851 a ship carrying passengers and a gold shipment sank near San Miguel. The captain abandoned ship and took the gold with him. One of the surviving passengers made it to the rocky island northwest of San Miguel Island and a passing ship rescued him. His name was Nathan Richardson, and apparently Richardson Rock was named for him.[12] After the 1850's no nineteenth-century stories of wrecks at the island were published with the exception of one about a small sheep boat, called the *Santa Rosa*. To date we have no real history of sailing vessels lost on or around the island. In the early twentieth century some dramatic accounts appeared, a few of which can be told here.

The Schooner *J.M Coleman,* Built in 1888

The competition between the Santa Fe and Southern Pacific Railroads in the late 1880's brought thousands of people out to live in California, setting off a huge building boom and a demand for northern lumber. The lumber ships maneuvered into the Santa Barbara Channel, and one of those that did not make it past San Miguel Island was the schooner, *J.M.Coleman*. The *Coleman* had set out from Everett, Washington with 800,000 feet of lumber aboard and on Sunday evening, August 30, 1905, ran into dense fog. It struck a sunken reef on the windy westward shore just inside Point Bennett and grounded itself on the rocks. Wedged between two of them, it was badly beaten by the waves. Mate Patterson and four sailors boarded a small row boat and set out for San Pedro. The Captain and four others remained on board awaiting help. The men in the row boat struggled against huge swells until they reached a point about sixteen miles off the coast where they were picked up by the Schooner *Mandalay*.

Point Bennett where the Coleman *went aground in 1988.*

Somehow Mate Patterson succeeded in dispatching a distress signal, and the Schooner *Chehalis* hurried to the rescue bringing officers of the J.A. Hooper Company, owners of the *J.M. Coleman*, to the scene. On September tenth, the fog was still so thick that coastwise vessels were endangered. The Schooner *Comet* narrowly missed drifting up onto the rocks next to the *Coleman* as she ventured blindly inside Richardson Reef. The large vessel, loaded with lumber, was saved when a timely breeze cleared the fog. On the 14th, the *Coleman*'s hull was still wedged between rocks with the prow to the sea. The bottom was gone, and other vessels could not come near to help save the rigging or transfer the lumber piled on the deck.

Finally, on September 26, 60,000 feet of lumber was transferred to a lighter, a small boat used for unloading, so it could be taken to a steamer, but it too was lost in a gale. Seamen remained with the wreck for three weeks longer hoping to tow her out, but she lay deep in the ocean and filled with water. When she was abandoned, her cargo of redwood lumber washed ashore. Much of it was later taken to the plateau above Cuyler Harbor and used to construct a new ranch house and sheep sheds.[13]

The Steamer *Anubis*

On July 18, 1908 the German steamer *Anubis* left San Francisco for Hamburg loaded with lumber, tallow, grain, flour, and sixty-eight people, many of them passengers. In a heavy fog the ship lost its bearings and was drawn off her course by heavy seas. She went aground on rocks a half mile east of Castle Rock on the west end of San Miguel Island. As the *Anubis* settled on the rocks the in-rushing water extinguished the fires under the boilers and the vessel took on a sharp list. The crew set to work heaving part of the deck load overboard to lighten her, and Captain von Salzen ordered seven of the crew to row a boat to Point Conception and get help. The course of the *Anubis* had been laid well outside the island, but something went wrong with the reckoning. Captain von Salzen claimed later that his compass was off. The *Santa Barbara Morning Press* headline on July 23rd read, "Swelling Grain May Burst Ship Asunder." Wide cracks appeared in the decks, and the ship was considered lost.

The vessel had gone through a half mile of densely woven kelp before she struck, so there she lay surrounded by kelp and deep water. On the 23rd nine persons went to the mainland in a life boat. The remainder were rescued and landed on the island where they camped in an improvised sailcloth tent. By then the hold had sixteen feet of water. This news was sent to Santa Barbara just as Captain Frank Nidever and a group of seal hunters arrived at the wreck on the power schooner *Ynez*. They had been in camp on San Miguel Island on the day the *Anubis* struck the ledge, heard the commotion, but the fog was so heavy that even though they sailed out within 200 yards of the ship, they had missed her. Meanwhile the ship lay steady, the water in her hold keeping her as quiet as a ship at anchor, and the rocks protecting her from high seas. The stern sank slightly. On the 27th divers went down and reported a number of small holes and a good many sheared rivets in the bottom, but prospects were good for floating the ship and replacing the broken steel plates. The steamer *Fulton* took on 450 tons of the cargo and the steamer *Dee Westport* also took cargo to San Francisco. On July 29th the crew pumped out the forward and after holds, lifted out the freight, and hauled her off the sunken

Channel Islands National Park

Castle Rock. When ships ground into these rocks the lumber from them piled up onshore.

ledge with anchor cables attached to the tug *Goliath*. The ship still had ten water-tight compartments fore and aft, the water being mostly amidship. At Cuyler Harbor she was patched up and then towed to San Francisco. The *Anubis* was the first ship to have been pulled off and saved at the Islands and also the largest to have been wrecked there. Happily for the Santa Barbarans, a local firm sifted, cleaned, and repacked a large quantity of the high grade flour on board and sold it to them at bargain prices.[14]

Schooner *Comet* Built in 1896

The *Comet* carrying lumber from Gray's Harbor, Washington to San Pedro ground its hull into Richardson Rock as it attempted to run the channel on the dark night of August 30, 1911. Later that night it drifted ashore at Simonton Cove. Captain Borgenson left eight crew members on board and set out in a row boat for Santa Barbara arriving there two days later. On September 14 Captain Short, the master of a power launch, found the wreckage stranded on a shoal with 200 to 300 yards of breakers between it and the open sea. The masts had snapped, the rigging was hopelessly tangled, and the ship and cargo were a total loss.

Salvage crews coming upon the scene asked the resident sheep rancher, Captain William Waters, who considered himself King of San Miguel Island, for permission to work from the shore side. Waters refused them permission. Since salvage was impossible from the seaward approach, Waters bought all salvaging rights for only $1,000 and carried lumber and useful items up to his ranch house.

In 1962 Richard Headley, a sea lion catcher on the island, came upon some pieces of the wreck, but by 1973 most of the *Comet* was buried in the beach at Simonton Cove. Only the anchor was exposed. The U.S. Navy has now forbidden wreck divers to excavate and remove any part of the ship. This is because San Miguel Island is protected under the Antiquities Act. Whole sections of the ship emerged from the sand in 1984.[15]

Schooner *Watson A. West* Built in 1901

Sailing from Aberdeen, Washington to San Pedro, California, the *Watson A. West* attempted to navigate east of Point Conception in a dense fog and crashed head on into the rock-toothed west end of San Miguel Island on February 24, 1923. The ship broke at the first impact and struck so hard that crew members were thrown out of their bunks. The cargo of lumber allowed the boat to float just long enough for the crew to make their escape in the life boats before the *Watson A. West* sank. Heading for the mainland, the men rowed all night and the next day without food or water. The following night they arrived at the foot of State Street in Santa Barbara exhausted, hungry, and half clad. The local newspaper noted that it was a miracle that the men had made it through the waves along the channel, claiming it was only the second time in history it had been done. Captain Sorenson had been with the ship since its launching twenty-two years before. Lumber from the *Watson A. West* washed ashore and eventually contributed to the fencing and out-buildings of the San Miguel ranch complex.[16]

The Steamer *Cuba*

The wreck of the *Cuba* is often tied to the loss of the seven U.S. Navy destroyers that careened into the rocks at Honda the night of September 7, 1923. Both accidents followed upon a strong earthquake in Japan, a quake that disturbed tides across the Pacific for many days. In the case of the destroyers the captain of the lead ship, believing he was south of Point Conception, gave orders for the turn to an easterly heading too soon and crashed into the rocks north of Point Arguello. Six more destroyers followed suit before the catastrophe was halted. The captain was actually fifteen miles north of Santa Barbara Channel. Whether this misreading was related to the earthquake has never been established, nor has the miscalculated heading of the *Cuba*.

The Pacific Mail steamship *Cuba*, bound north from Mazatlan to San Francisco struck the rocks at Point Bennett about 4:15 a.m. on September 8, 1923. The master had obtained a good noon position on September 7th and had laid his course to pass about two or three miles west of Point Bennett. He gave orders to be called so as to have ample time to check his bearings with the Richardson Rock Light, but he was still in bed when she grounded. Apparently, both the Third and Second Officers on watch had been ordered to call the captain in case of thick weather, but they later claimed they could see at all times for a distance of from two to three miles. The Lighthouse Service suggested that the disastrous heading might have been due either to careless steering or to a failure to allow for existing wind or possible leeway due to the sea.[17]

The *Cuba's* generator had broken down some time prior to the accident, so Captain Holland was not able to send out an S.O.S. call. At dawn some forty passengers were put ashore in life boats while others were sighted and taken on by a Navy torpedo boat which had survived the mass grounding at Honda the previous night. The *Cuba* was loaded with coffee, but the cargo was under water so long that it could not be salvaged. The vessel was advertised for sale and brought $700.[18]

Baby Bounty and the *Bounty* Barge

This modern entry under shipwrecks shifts from lumber schooners and steamships missing their way around Point Bennett to the unique problems of making a movie in San Miguel's waters. In 1935 Producer Irving Thalberg put his talent to work on one of the greatest sea stories ever filmed: *Mutiny On The Bounty*. To film it he planned several locations. A camera crew went to Tahiti twice for the crowd shots and scenic background. The major scenes were shot on Catalina, and for rough seas he chose the waters off San Miguel Island. He sent out an old 200 foot three-master with the outside reworked to match the ship design of the period and shot footage for a storm sequence; but the pitch and toss of the angry ocean was not convincing. Then someone suggested that they build a

Palm trees at Cuyler Harbor, probably introduced for the filming of Mutiny on the Bounty.

small model of the *Bounty* so that the contrast with the large waves would produce more drama. The result was the *Baby Bounty*, an eighteen-foot exact replica, just big enough to hold two men to steer it. It was towed to sea by the mother ship, and all the crew was sworn to secrecy so that the public would never know the difference. Finding heavy seas off San Miguel was no problem, and they began to shoot. Soon, however, the strong currents separated *Baby* from the larger *Bounty* and the small ship disappeared. Afraid to call the Coast Guard because the story could get into the newspapers, Thalberg hired several private ships to comb the waters. Two nights later the *Baby Bounty* and its two occupants were rescued.

Thalberg was doubly alarmed by the missing *Baby Bounty* incident because he had already lost an assistant cameraman while they were shooting a scene on a barge.

The barge was a good-sized affair with a replica of the stern of the *Bounty* built on one end of it. By taking on ballast at the other end, they could cause the partial replica to tip up and down as it if were about to sink. The cameraman, Glen Strong, was working with his camera on a tripod when the barge was suddenly swamped by a wave which washed his equipment and some valuable footage overboard. In attempting to save the equipment, Strong was drowned.[19] In spite of these calamities, San Miguel's waters helped in the production of a memorable sea film which won the Best Picture of the Year Award in 1935.

The *Tortuga*

The wreck of the *Tortuga* in December, 1987 was perhaps less of an event than the above since no people were aboard this Navy Landing Ship Dock (LSD). Its steel hull, however, may be visible at the island for many years to come. The *Tortuga* had been laid up for about 20 years, then filled with heavy debris it was used as a target ship.

Lois Roberts

The shipwrecked Tortuga *down under at Active Point.*

In late 1987, the Navy, wishing to run a test on a missile, closed up its 44 compartments and planted a special radar finding device on the LSD so that the missile could home in on it and sink it by impact. The missile had no warhead. It was close to Christmas, and a major storm was forecast; but in spite of this plans went ahead. Tow boats took the ship out beyond San Miguel Island, let it go, and the missile was shot off. It went in from the stern and came to rest on the bow. The LSD remained afloat thanks to all the metal debris on board which absorbed the shock of the missile. The Navy then decided to bomb the ship, but while they applied for the necessary permits the impending storm hit the California coast.

By daybreak the *Tortuga* had hit the rocks at Active Point on the southeast end of the island. Eighty feet of the stern broke off, an area that had been weakened before, and finally the whole stern was under water. Two large portions of the ship caught in the rocks had to be trimmed down by a salvage crew so that they could be left in place without disturbing the eye. During salvage operations, twelve-foot waves swamped the whole structure, leaving only short intervals between sets for the workers to apply their torches. The divers were the brave ones in this event: wet all day as they clung to the wreckage, and forced to swim out to sea beyond the rocks before they could attempt to come ashore at a distant beach. At last San Miguel Island had a shipwreck in full view.[20]

These unrelated accounts, each a drama in itself, constitute but a short list of the steam and sailing vessels lost around the island. Pieced together, they enable us to envision the challenges met by sailors who rounded Point Conception a century ago.

Navigational Aids

Mariners had been on their own until 1854 when the U.S. Lighthouse Board installed a strong beam at Point Conception. For the rest of the nineteenth century this was all ships had for guidance at the northwest end of the channel. San Miguel Island was not even reserved for lighthouse purposes until 1909, Richardson Rock until 1911, and Prince Island at the entrance to Cuyler Harbor until 1917. When, in 1911, the Navy sent out a circular letter asking for opinions from shippers and marine underwriters as to where the Lighthouse Service should spend money first, Anacapa Island or Richardson Rock, they chose the Rock. The responses argued that prevailing northwest coastal winds drove vessels past Point Conception in foggy weather and into the dangerous water near Richardson Rock.[21]

The Lighthouse Board proposed a beacon and a powerful fog signal for Richardson Rock. Yet, when Congress allotted the funds that year Anacapa Island was awarded a skeletal light tower and a whistling buoy while Richardson Rock got only a lighted whistle buoy. The buoy was anchored in 270 feet of water northwest of the rock and projected sixteen feet above water. In 1911 another bell-buoy was anchored in 120 feet of water off the southwest end of San Miguel Island, but the enormous quantities of kelp frequently fouled and capsized it. Ships passing outside the island on their way along the coast claimed they never heard or saw it. So, since it was virtually useless, it was discontinued in 1918. Navigation between Point Conception and San Miguel Island continued to be the greatest threat to shipping bound between San Francisco and Los Angeles.

Ships sailing from Central and South America to San Francisco invariably passed outside of San Miguel Island because it saved them 25 to 30 miles over the inside course. This kind of traffic took the inside course only in heavy weather because then it offered shelter from the southeast wind and Pacific storms. In 1923, while pursuing the outside course, the *Cuba* had been wrecked on San Miguel while rounding Point Bennett on the westerly side. This generated a flurry of requests, especially from the Pacific Mail and Steamship Company, for a lighthouse on the westerly side of the island, and a demand for immediate installation of a gas and whistling buoy at Point Bennett.

New hydrographic readings were made outside the kelp beds at the Point and a buoy was placed about three hundred feet off the tip of the island in November, 1924.

By the 1940's the Richardson Rock buoy was considered so important that even during the blackouts of World War II, it was only inoperative for six days. In 1948 it was rebuilt eleven yards from the Rock. Wartime traffic finally forced the Service to build a white skeletal tower at about the middle of the south side of the island near Crooks Point. That light flashed 75 times a minute until it was discontinued in 1953.[22]

Instrumentation and sophisticated navigational aids have made the big shipwrecks at Point Bennett a thing of the past. Small craft, however, still respect or avoid the northwest entrance to the Santa Barbara Channel and the pounding surf on San Miguel's west end. Driving along Highway 101 one rarely sees a small sail on the horizon there.

Chapter VII

SHEEP RANCHING ON SAN MIGUEL ISLAND

As early as 1850 Americans used the island for sheep ranching. Its ten thousand acres, several springs, and lush covering of native vegetation made it ideal. Moreover, a herder was hardly necessary with the sea as a barrier on all sides. Sheep came to the California mainland with the Franciscan missionaries, and herds persisted through the Mexican period when some were introduced to the islands of Santa Rosa and Santa Cruz. Then, with the coming of the Americans and decline in the Mexican hide and tallow trade, hundreds of thousands of sheep were driven on overland trails to the coastal valleys. As public domain the offshore islands became increasingly popular for sheepmen who wanted to run sheep at no cost. One man who took advantage of the opportunity was Samuel C. Bruce. He had sheep on San Miguel Island for some time prior to 1850, though he preferred to describe his presence as a possessory right to the island itself. Possibly discouraged by the treacherous access to the island, he sold his interests to the famous mountain man and hunter, George Nidever.[1]

The George Nidever Era

Nidever, it will be recalled, came to Santa Barbara to hunt otters in 1835. In 1840 he bought the original Mission House adobe at the harbor from another American, Joseph Chapman. It stood on a low mound at the foot of present-day State Street and was later named after a subsequent owner, Lewis Burton. The Burton Mound adobe was the most conspicuous feature on the Santa Barbara waterfront for seventy years. A mill stood beside it, and it was so centrally located that petitions addressed to the Mexican Town Council commonly used the "Naidivar place by the old saltery" as a survey point when describing land claims in the city.[2]

George Nidever married Sinforosa Sanchez, the daughter of a Mexican Don in 1841. Her father was grantee to the 14,000 acre Rancho Santa Clara Rio del Norte, so Sinforosa grew up among Santa Barbara's best families. She would share her graceful living and valuable connections with her new husband.

Nidever stayed on land for over two years during this period. Then he went out on Alpheus B. Thompson's boat with other hunters. He had to charter ships or hunt for otters off the land since he had no boat, and he divided his time between his growing family, hunting grizzly bears, and the sea. In 1850 he worked as a pilot on a U.S. Coast Survey boat for Capt. James Alden making a survey around San Miguel. Right after that job he went to San Francisco and bought a seventeen-ton schooner for himself.[3] When he brought it back to the Santa Barbara Channel, he had the only boat around large enough to take the rough seas of the channel's outer rim, and he could even sail out as far as San Nicholas Island. He could take on perilous seas with his new boat, and this may account

Channel Islands National Park

Captain George Nidever.

Bill Roberts

Exposed rafters of the old ranch adobe. Nidever's two sons tired of living here.

for his buying out Bruce's sheep ranch on San Miguel that year. He and his wife continued to live in Santa Barbara close to her large family, and it is unlikely that Sinforosa ever set foot on the island.

Like the other absentee ranch owners in the city, Nidever probably sent a herder or manager out to care for his livestock. But his best friend, Carl Dittman whom he called Charley Brown, mentioned once that Nidever did leave the hunt to go out to San Miguel for the winter's work. His sons, George and Mark, who were under ten years old when he bought the ranch, eventually went out to live there. They used a small adobe house above Cuyler Harbor possibly built by Bruce or with their help. While their parents enjoyed the city's social life and their father sailed his schooner, the young men endured isolation along with the excitement of living in a wilderness. They soon tired of the place, urging their father to sell it, but despite setbacks, sheep raising was profitable, and Nidever had no desire to dispose of his island. When his sons finally did leave, the adobe was abandoned to the elements. Its ruins, a few exposed rafters and wall stubs, still survive close to a gully.[4]

For Nidever, San Miguel started out as a highly lucrative venture. In 1850, he had stocked the island with 45 sheep, 17 cattle, 2 hogs, and 7 horses, paying only $10 for the sheep. Twelve years later, and from this original stock, he had 6,000 sheep, 200 cattle, 100 hogs, and 32 horses![5] But his bonanza was not destined to last.

Meanwhile, early in his ownership of San Miguel, Nidever played a prominent part in a legendary bit of Indian lore. Everyone up and down the coast of California knew the story of the woman who had been left behind on San Nicholas Island, when in 1836 the Mission fathers had ordered the evacuation of all Indians from that remote piece of land. Removal had been accomplished by means of a chartered schooner, which could not tarry to search for the woman, and none of the smaller local boats dared venture into the channel's rough seas. Over the ensuing years, few people believed that she could have survived. Then, in 1852, while on a trip to the island to hunt seagull eggs, Nidever and his companions came upon human footprints. A sudden gale forced them to make a speedy departure, but they returned the following July. Tracing footmarks, they spotted the woman on a small ridge and quickly surrounded her so that she would not escape. To their amazement, she showed no alarm. Bowing and smiling, she even offered them some roasted roots to eat. Clothed in a robe fashioned of cormorant feathers, she appeared to be in good physical condition despite her long, lonely ordeal.

Once she understood that they wished her to go with them, she carefully packed some seal meat, a seal's head, and other of her things in baskets and went aboard ship for dinner. When Nidever's friend, Charley Brown, made her a dress out of some ticking, a man's shirt, and a black neck tie she wore it with delight, and during the month the men hunted from the island she worked with her baskets and showed a great interest in all they did. She found them quite wasteful, and once she dragged a skinned otter carcass out of the surf and onto the beach saving it there till Nidever's men could no longer stand the stench and threw it back into the water. She also hoarded bones, taking them out from her basket to suck over and over again.[6]

The woman returned with the men to Santa Barbara where half the town came out to see her. She delighted everyone with her good humor, singing, and dancing. But civilization proved too great a challenge. Within five weeks she was ill, and in the seventh week, she died. On her death bed, she was baptized by a priest from the Santa Barbara Mission and buried in the Mission graveyard. Her rough casket had been built by Nidever, before he left on another sailing trip. The feathered robe was sent to Rome, where it is housed in the Vatican Museum.

For over a decade, Nidever continued to reap rich rewards from his island venture. Then, in 1864, the halcyon days came to an end. The Great Drought of 1863-64, which caused mainland ranchers to lose half their stock, proved disastrous for Nidever. His six thousand sheep were already well over twice the number the island's native flora could sustain. The dry north winds, unseasonable heat, and a whole winter without rain forced the under-nourished animals to consume every bush and tree, even tear up roots, and then face starvation. Five thousand perished, 83 percent of Nidever's herd.[7]

In 1869, his sons finally got their way, when Nidever reluctantly sold his island, stock, and improvements to Hiram W. Mills, receiving somewhere between ten and fifteen thousand dollars. He next made real estate investments in Montecito, Casitas Pass, Sycamore Canyon, and Carpenteria. In 1876, an interviewer working under the great California historian Hubert H. Bancroft found him farming his Carpenteria property.[8] At seventy nine, his life of adventure was over. But his qualities of skill, ingenuity, and courage made him a symbolic figure—the archetype of those first Americans who broke through the west all the way to California during the Mexican era. He died in 1878, outliving by far most of the reckless breed of

Mountain Men with whom he came over the Rockies in the 1830's.

Nidever apparently looked upon San Miguel mainly for its economic potential as did some of his successors. In his time men prided themselves upon surviving the environment, not saving it. Since the first botanist to visit the island and catalogue its plant communities came in 1887, we may never know the nature of its lush primal vegetation. But in the spring of 1871, when pasture should have been at its finest, Stehman Forney, working on a U.S. Coast Survey team, wrote that San Miguel was covered with coarse grasses, devoid of a single tree, and without underbrush of any kind. In 1875, the archaeologist, Paul Schumaker, also reported ruined vegetation and sheep being led to the shearing shed in a starving condition. He called the island a barren lump of sand.[9]

The Waters Regency

The new owners, Hiram Mills and his brother Warren, belonged to the age of enterprise, of corporations, and city business connections. They put title to the island under the Pacific Wool Growing Co. based in San Francisco, while they speculated on land in Lompoc Valley and Montecito and hired managers to care for the island ranch. Warren came out to the island sporadically, and the brothers built a small two-story house near the Cuyler Harbor arroyo just east of the ruined old adobe. The wool market collapsed in 1876 but they hung on for a decade, when Warren announced that he was tired of the island and would never come out there again. In November, 1887, they sold a half interest in the island to a San Franciscan named William G. Waters, and continued to look for a buyer for the other half.[10]

When Waters bought San Miguel he was living modestly with his wife on Post Street in San Francisco, but they were both originally from Massachusetts. She had come to California in 1859 with her first husband and was widowed in 1873. William had fought in the Civil War and then had come out west. They married in 1880. We do not know how Waters earned a living, but Mrs. Waters revealed in her diary that she put up the $10,000 to pay for the island ranch, writing, "I knew Will had nothing and I wanted to hold him."[11] Beyond this insecurity, Mrs. Waters had tuberculosis with severe hemorrhages. Once the papers were signed, the couple hastened to Santa Barbara and on to San Miguel hoping the climate there would bring about a cure. Will also saw the venture as a chance in a lifetime to make some money.

On January 1, 1888 the couple sailed out to San Miguel Island taking along Mrs. Waters's fourteen-year-old adopted daughter Edith, a woman servant Ida, and a hired man, Adolph. A younger man, Jimmie, who had already worked on the island for several months, met them at Cuyler Harbor and took everyone to the west end of the island to celebrate their New Year's Day arrival. To accomodate Mrs. Waters and Ida, he fastened two rocking chairs to a large sled harnessed to a pair of donkeys while Edith, Will, and Adolph followed on horseback. Jimmie showed them a fresh water spring, and the men gathered abalone for supper. That evening as they sat in the warm kitchen in the house Mills had built, everyone looked forward to the months ahead. Will loved the outdoors, and with his helpers this city man took on the hard work of planting, building roads, repairing buildings, and caring for 4,000 sheep as well as 30 head of cattle and horses. Edith was to have a pet lamb and her own mule to ride, and Mrs. Waters would ride horseback, visit beaches and watch the men work.

As it turned out, there were many days on which Mrs. Waters could not leave the house because of the wind, the island's distinctive weather factor. This Mrs. Waters recorded daily in the diary which she meticulously kept: "some wind, furious north wind, gale force, blowing all night, harder than ever, wind part of day," or in one notable entry "no wind today." Fog hung over the island and occasional rains left the house in a small basin of sticky adobe mud. Their home was a crude two-story structure built partially from railroad ties, with a bunk house, shearing shed, and blacksmith shop nearby. But despite discomforts and the fact that Mrs. Waters endured chronic pain and a general weakness that often kept her in bed till noon, Will's enthusiasm for the ranch, along with his kindness to his wife and her love for him, established a great harmony shared by the entire island family.

Immediately after their arrival, the men had begun to plant grain in the big meadow above the house, fenced off from the south side of the island where the sheep had been turned out. By mid-February they had sown over fifty sacks of grain and planted an additional twenty acres of barley. Plentiful rain that winter brought forth good crops, and in addition, Waters grew his own potatoes, built a grape arbor, and supplemented their diet with fish and abalone. Tough fried abalone and salt pork for the everyday breakfast and abalone soup for dinner were the family's customary daily fare.

Waters, Adolph, and Jimmie completed several projects during their stay: a new barn floor to keep grain out of the reach of multitudes of island mice, a tool house, new fences, and by far the most ambitious—the new road down to the beach and over to the boat house at the dock. Waters and his crew blasted out rocks for several weeks on this undertaking, but in the end it was too narrow. Perched along the side of a fifty-foot deep arroyo it was always plagued with slides and washouts. Mrs. Waters rode down the incline in a dog cart one day and wrote that she was scared to death. Rain and mud rarely kept the men from work. They toiled in gales that swept sand over the island the whole day long.

Simple pleasures filled their evening hours: card games such as Euchre and Pedro, reading aloud to each other, and occasionally Mrs. Waters sang for the group or provided the thrill of a seance conducted around the dining table. At these sessions Edith learned that she had once been incarnated as a French countess, Mrs. Waters that she had been a Russian peasant, and the hired man, Adolph, was appalled to find that "he was formerly a

Hebrew and the third judge on the Danhedrin [Sanhedrin] that tried Christ." He lost interest in the seances after that.

Each Sunday outing was an adventure as they set out on the sled and by horseback to discover distant bays and grassy meadows. Once it was to the base of Green Mountain where they collected mustard greens and the most beautiful wild flowers they had ever seen. At the beaches they fished and hunted shellfish and larger game. On one occasion Will killed three seals for their skins and Adolph shot a bald eagle with a seven-and-a-half foot wing span. Another Sunday they rowed out to Gull Island (also known as Prince Island) to picnic and fish. For Mrs. Waters it was an exhausting climb up the rocks, but worth it to eat their simple lunch there amidst the beautiful surroundings. All their adventures were carefully recorded in her diary, as were their many vicissitudes.

All days were not carefree. Flour ran out, and the schooner with supplies and mail could be held up by the weather for weeks beyond its target date of every six weeks to two months. The rare sight of a strange schooner was warning that poachers might be landing in some cove to take away their sheep. The island fox ate the turkeys and their young, and birds ruined the vegetable garden. Mrs. Waters lived in constant fear of the roof blowing off, and the dull foggy days drove her into depressions. Justifiably concerned with death, she recorded talks with old friends "on the other side of the river." Her diary is a page out of nineteenth-century women's history, the classic invalid and dutiful wife: shy, frustrated, and busy with little tasks such as rearranging her closet, mending sheets, and making a scrapbook out of clippings from *Harpers Magazine*. Now it is remarkable to find that it is only through her writing that we can find out anything about the intimacies of nineteenth century ranch life on San Miguel Island. Intermittent hemorrhages continued so that both she and Will knew the island life had not effected a cure. It was time for them to leave.

Mr. W. I. Nichols became Waters' partner when he bought the interest belonging to Warren Mills in early

Robert Brooks Collection

William G. Waters, King of the Island and architect of the ranch house.

February. Mills brought Nichols out to San Miguel on February 16 to meet Waters. That evening they made an arrangement for Nichols to send out a ranch manager on May 29, 1888. Thus, at the end of May a Mr. Read came, with his wife and six children, to manage the ranch. To support his family Read would receive a third of the stock increase each year. The Waters were free to leave and were back in Santa Barbara on June 2. Waters shaved off his beard, cut his hair, and donned his mainland clothes. After a few weeks they boarded the coast train at the railhead in San Luis Obispo. Mrs. Waters died in San Francisco on January 17, 1890.

The San Miguel Ranch was profitable business in 1890. The value of the house, barn, mowing machines, several vessels used at the dock, and of the stock itself comprised part of its worth. The other part was, until then, the unchallenged possessory right to the island that the ranchers deeded to each other. Mr. Nichols sold his interest in the island to William Schilling of Long Beach December 19, 1889 for $10,000, but Waters became possessed with the idea of owning and ruling the whole island. He returned to live on San Miguel after his wife's death with her adopted daughter, Edith. Edith was a teenager, hated San Miguel, and claimed she was a prisoner on an island swept by perpetual gales. She finally fled to the mainland on a boat that had come out to gather guano.[12]

In December 1890 Waters apparently became the sole owner of the island and signed a promissory note for $7,000 made out to his partner, Schilling, giving as security all of his personal property on San Miguel. These included 3,000 sheep, 150 cattle more or less, hogs, poultry, goats, miscellaneous tools and buildings, and the sloop *Liberty*. In January 1892 Schilling transferred the note to Elias Beckman, a financier of Ventura. On February 4, 1897, Waters, giving San Miguel as his residence, and four Los Angeles men formed the San Miguel Island Company incorporating with a capital stock of $50,000. They claimed the island and all on it their exclusive possession.[13] The island had never been a Mexican land grant and thus had never cleared title through the Land Claims Commission. Nor had it ever been subject to a cadastral survey or patented in the U.S. Land Office. Possessory right to the land had been passed around and duly recorded in the deed books since the time of Bruce. Now, Elias Beckman who held Waters' note was sophisticated enough to want a distinction made between personal property and title to the land. When news of the San Miguel Island Company reached him he filed a case to block transfer of the island to the Company and went to court in 1908. The General Land Office was called in for guidance, and it confirmed that no land claim had ever been filed for the island. The Company was dissolved with possessory rights distributed among the stockholders, and Waters soon became the sole possessor.[14]

William Waters had known of the cloud over the title and had extended the cloud to include the question of sovereignty as early as 1895. That year newspapers ran an item reporting that England could take San Miguel Island for a coaling station since it had not been mentioned in the Treaty of Guadalupe Hidalgo which settled the Mexican

War in 1848. Perhaps because of the English menace, President Grover Cleveland sent out surveyors under the United States marshal Nicholas Covarruias in July 1896. Waters met the marshal on the beach, protested his entry, but did not resist the order.[15] Previous to this call he had sent several U.S. survey parties on their way. Waters retold the story of the confrontation with the marshal to Mrs. Trask, an island visitor in 1906. He called himself the King of San Miguel and informed her that "he had purchased the island from a Mexican to whom the island had come as a Spanish grant; and that it never had been formally taken possession of by the United States."[16] He spoke of how often he had turned his cannon on an officer who came without necessary official papers but explained that when Grover Cleveland had sent a civil request as the head of one nation made to another, the King of San Miguel Island had very gallantly turned the freedom of the island over to his men.

In 1906 William Waters commenced work on the largest ranch house ever built on an off-shore California island. By this time he also had a full-time resident manager named John Russell. The house was a monumental task in which Waters, still a vigorous man in his sixties, took an active part. Waters sailed into Santa Barbara to get materials and to describe its progress to newspaper reporters. He used the first person as if to make it known that he indeed designed it and was building it displaying the tremendous enthusiasm he had always had for ranch projects.

Rejecting the protection of the arroyo where the sand-covered remnants of the Mills house stood, Waters chose to place his house on the meadow six hundred feet above Cuyler Harbor. To fend off potential hundred mile an hour winds, he constructed a 120 foot double-wall on the side angled to the northwest with port holes for windows. Along it he built eight large rooms all opening out onto a long porch facing the southeast. The residents could also go from the kitchen, room to room, inside thanks to sliding doors. Using doors that slid right into the wall rather than swinging doors was quite an innovation

Betsy Lester Roberti

Waters' ranch house and out-buildings, 1938.

for a turn-of-the-century house. The eight rooms included five bedrooms, each with running water and set wash bowls, two dining rooms, so the shearers could eat separately, and a large kitchen. In addition, the main building housed a wash room, milk room, and meat room. Apart from this in a separate "L" shaped structure about ninety feet long, Waters maintained carpenter and blacksmith shops, a harness room, cow barn, and storage space for wagons and tools. Toward the arroyo stood the shearing house, sheep shed and corrals, and in the arroyo was a good well and a windmill which forced water up to the house which was 125 feet away on higher land.[17]

Much of the wood for the ranch complex came from shipwrecks and from the cargoes of lumber schooners that had come to grief on the west end of the island. For example, the *J.M. Coleman* had gone aground in 1905 just inside Point Bennett. The men hauled the redwood lumber it carried from the ship up to the ranch house site on Mexican burros. Flour in twill bags also washed ashore. John Russell later recalled that they piled the bags of flour on top of the lumber before hauling it up the hill. The wet sacks sealed the flour tight, and the Russells used the flour for years. As lumber drifted ashore from ships like the *Comet* and the *J.F. West,* the house was reinforced, fences and outbuildings repaired. A warehouse and wharf on the beach below completed the ranch complex, the whole a tribute to Waters' ingenuity and consuming drive. The *Santa Barbara News Press* reported on his house as being comparable to any Mediterranean resort.[18]

In 1911 when Waters spelled out his improvements for the Lighthouse District Office he emphasized his personal involvement in the house. This is emphasized here because after Waters' death some called the Ranch House John Russell's project, but this would not be credible. Today the site is called the Lester Ranch, another puzzling misnomer.

Assuredly, Waters' sheep business brought him considerable affluence. Still, throughout his long tenure he gained the reputation of a man who could nearly always be found on the island. Mainly because he claimed to own the island as a kingdom, he was regarded as somewhat peculiar. By 1909 he was known along the Santa Barbara Channel as "Captain" Waters and ran about 5,000 sheep. John Russell's presence on the island allowed Waters some freedom, and he belonged to the Jonathan Clubs of San Francisco and Los Angeles. He was also running into legal problems in his claim to the island kingdom.

In 1909 President Taft signed a bill reserving the island for lighthouse purposes under the Department of Commerce. Waters protested, arguing that he had lived on the island since 1887, made improvements, and that no mention had been made of the island in the treaty recognizing Mexico's independence from Spain or in the treaty ending the Mexican-American War. The Department of Commerce responded by offering him a five-year lease to the island, at five dollars a year. Other would-be lessees protested, and Waters readily accepted. Lighthouse personnel came to inspect the water supply and to judge whether the rate of flow could furnish power for a future lighthouse. Waters took them around the island graciously showing them all the springs. He renewed his lease in 1916.[19]

Meanwhile, pleasure craft and sports fishermen had begun to visit the island and some of these observers were disturbed by the serious damage caused by overgrazing. Waters ran about 5,000 sheep, two to three times the number the forage could safely support. Articles were published and letters addressed to the government. The Department of Commerce was petitioned by a Montana rancher, offering to remove the sheep for two years, while he planted grasses and hardy trees. The Audubon Society applied for permission to turn the island into a bird refuge. Both requests were rejected on the basis that not only ranchers but also the community at large derived certain benefits from the grazing industry. The Audubon Society was offered Prince Island.[20]

Robert L. Brooks, The Last Lessee

In April, 1917, William Waters, pioneer developer of San Miguel Island, died of a stroke.[21] He had lived on the island for almost thirty years and had put more of his own physical labor into its development than would any other man. Just four months prior to his death, he had sold his interest in the island, including all ranch improvements and 1,700 Merino sheep, to a twenty-five-year-old mainland rancher named Robert L. Brooks and his partner J. R. Moore. After some debate, the Lighthouse Bureau decided to lease San Miguel to Brooks and Moore for $200 a year. In 1918 the ranch sheared 2,391 sheep. Both Brooks and Moore had served in the army during World War I and in their absence arranged for the Vail brothers who owned a ranch on the neighboring island of Santa Rosa to help out. John Russell continued on as manager. Brooks was overseas for 21 months. Upon discharge the two lessees turned their attention to the island. Holding that maximum production and island regeneration could only be accomplished with a long-term lease, they had a bill drawn

Robert Brooks Collection

Robert L. Brooks, center, thrived on hard outdoor work with his ranch hands.

up to place before Congress which would assign the Brooks and Moore partnership a twenty-five year lease at $400 a year. In return, they would invest $10,000 in improvements outlined in the bill. Accordingly they would take measures to control the 5,000-acre sand pit which ran across the island and replant grasses, thus saving up to 2,000 acres. Brooks argued that the $400 per annum rental translated into heads of sheep would mean an annual cost of 20 cents per sheep, high pay for public grazing land on the mainland. Brooks' progressive policy was turned down by Superintendent Rhodes. Rhodes claimed that annual grazing costs were a cent a day ($3.65 per annum) per head on the mainland; the rental was too low.[22]

Robert Brooks was a mainland rancher and probably knew grazing costs as well as anyone. He was a handsome and colorful man who had first come to California as a result of an enforced year away from his studies at Yale University. During Easter vacation, 1911, he and some classmates had boarded a freighter and gone to London.

Deciding they would never make it back in time for classes one of the boys wired his professor a flippant message to the effect that he should not hold up the class for his return. All of the vacationers were dismissed for a year. During this year Brooks came out to work on the ranch of an older brother, Philip, in the Imperial Valley. While he was there he met the Vails (of Santa Rosa Island) who were also farming in the Imperial Valley near Calipatria. The Vails told him of the system of island leases, so after graduation from Yale he made the deal with Waters. In 1918 Brooks returned from service in France, had an office in the Van Nuys Building in Los Angeles, and began to invest in rural real estate and crops such as sugar beets and lima beans. Brooks seemed like the kind of man whose optimism and general good sense could take him anywhere he wanted to go. He probably borrowed money to get started, but before long he married and lived on Camden Drive in Beverly Hills. He did not spend any significant amount of time indoors and instead worked around Oxnard and in Ventura County. After some talks with an old prep school friend named Butler who lived in the area, he bought a ranch in Camarillo in 1931, and gradually developed two ranches on the mainland. In 1942 he brought his family to Hilltop Ranch in Carpinteria.[23]

Brooks thrived on work, hard outdoor work where he rubbed elbows with the ranch hands. At the end of the day he loved to drink and talk and spin tales with them, and he kept pictures of himself and these friends. San Miguel Island provided perhaps half of his annual income, but the island was far more important than income to Brooks. It supplied the romance he needed, a place to talk about, and a place to go with his workers at shearing time. Shearing was a huge event, and the whole family got up in the middle of the night to see him off. In rounding up his supplies Brooks took along 30 gallons of wine and stopped in at a State Street cafe where he told the owner to fill a box with liquor, whatever he could not move. Work started before daybreak, and before each man's plate was a glass full of whiskey. His shearing hands consisted of several professional shearers and unskilled workers. He referred to the latter as "the bums of Santa Barbara." He cleared the county jail of inmates each year and claimed the city fathers loved him for it. Then he took his men out on Joe Castagnola's boat or Vail's *Vacquero*.

Brooks used the *Vacquero* to haul sheep, but later he used a tug, the *Rio Grande*, which pulled a World War II landing craft outfitted with decks to serve as a barge. Each year the old wharf had to be taken out to avoid wave damage and the lumber stored for the next year's use. Upon arrival Brooks and his helpers put in a new holding pen and new chutes to bring the sheep down to the wharf. The men building the wharf had to walk out on the rocks and feel for the holes where the old bolts were with their feet in order to install 4 x 4's. It was cold, but Mr. Brooks gave everyone a shot of whisky now and then to keep them warm and going. Shearing was tough too, as the sheep carried about an inch of sand packed next to their skin. Eventually those headed for the mainland would be loaded into the barge, 55 at a time, and taken to Port Hueneme, unloaded, and transferred to the Brooks ranch at Camarillo. Sheep grazing on San Miguel went well even though there were predators. Eagles carried off a good number of the new-born lambs and the island fox attacked them as well. Tax records indicate that none of the unsecured property on San Miguel was ever assessed. When, in 1923 San Miguel suffered a drought, Brooks took all the sheep out to San Nicolas Island where he got permission from E.N. Vail to run them for a year.[24]

John Russell and his wife stayed on as resident managers in the 1920's, but Brooks visited regularly and did much to improve the ranch facilities. He built a strong fence attached to the house at the west end but angled easterly to shelter the structure against drifting sands and southwest winds. With this the ranch structure took on an "A" shape.[25] Though Brooks was involved in numerous other successful ranching enterprises, San Miguel continued to be the primary focus of his energies. He never lived on San Miguel, but he knew it well and knew it longer than any other lessee or resident employee. In need of a new manager, in 1929, Brooks brought another man to the island, who was also destined to fall under its spell.

Herbert Steever Lester had served in the armed forces with Brooks during World War I, where the two men had become friends. Lester had suffered the effects of shell shock, and though mostly recovered, he needed to escape from the demands of life on the mainland. When Brooks offered him the job of ranch manager, after Russell resigned, Lester decided to give it a try. Thus ensued a fascinating interlude in the history of the island.[26]

Lester and his new bride, Elizabeth, initiated a totally new life-style on San Miguel. Her intellect and cultural interests, demonstrated by a 500 book library, together with Herbie's charm and ingratiating personality soon served as a magnet to draw celebrities as well as more mundane visitors to an island that heretofore had been known only for shipwrecks and grazing. Sports fishing and recreational sailing were on the rise, adding to the

Betsy Lester Roberti

Herbert Steever Lester, the Legendary King.

influx, and once the visitors went ashore they were treated to high tea embellished by Elizabeth's scintillating conversation, or partook of libations at Herbie's popular Killer Whale Bar. All became enthusiastic publicity agents for the Lester menage. Journalists followed in their wake, and articles about Rancho Rambouillet, as Lester called the island after a place he knew in France, were published on the front pages of California newspapers and in national periodicals. It was even fallaciously reported that the Merino sheep were French imports from the environs of Rambouillet.

For a while, San Miguel came to be known as Lester's Island, and following in Waters' footsteps, he too dubbed himself King of San Miguel, wearing a makeshift insignia to designate his rank. Mrs. Lester's charming book, *The Legendary King of San Miguel,* later provided an insight into both the glamour and everyday inconveniences of life on the island. As ranch activity was now restricted to sheep raising, the Lesters were dependent upon supplies from the mainland for virtually all their food. Moreover, hordes of mice threatened to ravage their store of staples. The quixotic Mr. Lester refused to allow the importation of cats to deal with the rodents on the theory that the white-footed mice were rare creatures, indigenous to the islands, and must be protected.

When the Lesters two little daughters, Marianne and Betsy, approached school age, the family pondered the question of where to enroll them in school. Sending them to the mainland was difficult to accept, so Mrs. Lester decided to teach them herself. The Vails, on the nearby island of Santa Rosa, sent over a small playhouse to serve as a schoolroom. The Lesters equipped it with child-sized desks, hung a ship's bell outside, and placed a picture of George Washington on the wall. When the bell was rung the girls and the Waters's old dog, Pomo, entered for a serious day's work. Fame soon spread about this unique arrangement, and in 1940 *Life Magazine* published an article about it entitled "Swiss Family Lester." Students in Santa Barbara researched the school for class projects and exchanged letters with the girls, thus bringing the island to the attention of Santa Barbara's younger generation for the first time even though it had always been just thirty miles offshore.

A frequent visitor to the island was George Fisk Hammond, an old friend of Robert Brooks, who owned a small private plane and enjoyed flying out to San Miguel from his ranch along the beach in Santa Barbara. From his first landing in July, 1934, he always received a very warm welcome from the Lesters as his arrival brought the bonanza of fresh groceries, vegetables and just plain treats. When he found that he could be of some service to them he flew out weekly. Hammond and Herbie laid out markers on an improvised landing field, which the U.S. Coast Survey team later entered on aeronautical charts as Hammond Field. This designation remained until 1965. Once Hammond became aware of the irregularity of the Lester's mail service, he took over the additional task of

Betsy Lester Roberti

The Lester family with pilot Hammond, Pomo the dog, and the sled, the island's basic transportation.

flying their mail from his ranch, where the U.S. Postal Service delivered it, transporting it in a canvas bag appropriately labeled, "Hammond Airmail, Kingdom of San Miguel Island." For at least eight years, this good Samaritan flew his single-engine plane for an hour at a time, often in wind and fog, to reach the island's rough landing field. But his pleasure came from what every pilot seeks—challenging flight for good reason.[27]

Betsy Lester Roberti

Robert Brooks serving Arno at the popular Killer Whale Bar.

Meanwhile, the hard-working Brooks came out to the island regularly to tend his sheep and to stay in the ranch house. In June of 1937, while working on reconstruction of the landing from which the lambs were loaded for market, he lost his footing and fell. He had been standing on some slippery rocks and pitched backward onto a rusted bolt which sank into the flesh of his thigh. He was in danger of bleeding to death if he did not receive immediate attention. His workers carried him up to the ranch house where Lester took quick action. Relying on his army experience, he sterilized the wound with Lysol and stitched it closed with a curved needle and some fishline. For Brooks it was a painful procedure as there was no anesthetic aside from alcohol. The ranch had no radio, and although a flag was hoisted upside down in the hope of attracting a passing vessel, it was not until two weeks later that the *Vacquero,* their regular supply ship, transported Brooks to the mainland where he spent several days at the Cottage Hospital under observation. Luckily no infection developed. But Brooks was irked by the hullabaloo in the press, with sensational headlines such as "Millionaire's Life Saved by Crude Surgery on Island." He hated being called a millionaire as he always perceived himself to be a working man making daily contacts with the hardest aspects of ranch life, even land poor. From his point of view a millionaire was a man in a black suit, conducting business in a plush office.[28]

While Brooks and the Lesters were enjoying their idyllic existence on the island, the halcyon days for sheep ranching on San Miguel were drawing to a close, doomed by both its unique park-like features and its strategic position off shore. On November 7, 1934, President Franklin Roosevelt transferred jurisdiction of the island from the Secretary of Commerce to the Secretary of the Navy. The order reserved select sites for navigational aids and the following year when Brooks signed his grazing lease, the number of sheep he could run was restricted to 1200. Under pressure from environmentalists the number was later changed to a thousand. The hardship of a

Robert Brooks Collection

Shearing time, 1946. Left to right top row seated: Robert L. Brooks, Tom Ashton and two other shearers. Standing: Manager Al "Whity" Baglin, Don Butler, "Frenchie" Hal Hogg, and Pilot Robbie Robinson.

resultant reduced income was compounded by an increase in the amount of the grazing fee to $600 annually. The fate of San Miguel became of even greater interest to environmentalists when President Roosevelt proclaimed Santa Barbara Island and Anacapa Island a National Monument in 1938. It seemed only a question of time before San Miguel would be included. The Park Service made a study of the island in 1939, concluding that all the sheep must be removed and that a replanting program should begin immediately.[29] But no action was taken. Then, World War II broke out, and plans for environmental protection were set aside.

The attack on Pearl Harbor in December, 1941 brought an overnight change in the lives of the Lester family. By Christmas they had two Navy men living with them and

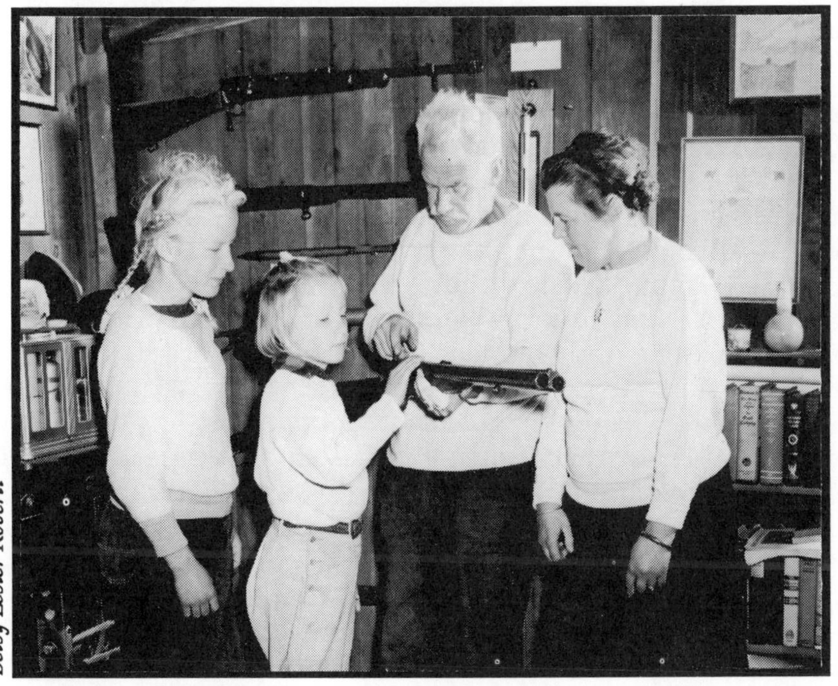

Betsy Lester Roberti

Herbie Lester showing Marianne, Betsy, and his wife Elizabeth his 425 double barrel elephant gun in the living room at Rancho Rambouillet, May, 1942, a month before tragedy struck.

they had been cut off from the mainland except for a short-wave radio and a Coast Guard supply boat. They were told they could either leave or stay at their own risk. Christmas passed without mail or presents for the girls. The situation took its toll on Herbie. Anxious and despondent, he was plagued by an old war wound, a hand injured when chopping wood, and by the side effects of sulpha drugs. That spring, while cutting wood, he chopped off two fingers and had to go to the mainland for treatment. After returning to the island he apparently waited for a day when he saw Brooks come into the harbor on the *Vaquero* . His family would not be alone. It was June 18, 1942, and he walked alone to a distant grassy spot and took his life with his Army 45.[30] Brooks and his companion, Don Butler, built a coffin for him and buried him on Devils Point where he had chosen to die.[31] The Lester's twelve years of idyllic existence had terminated in tragedy.

The good years had also run out for Brooks, but he persevered. He hired an old Norwegian sailor and his wife, Ulmar and Rae Englund, as resident managers after Lester's death. Rae cooked for the crew as had the other wives; her specialty being griddle-sized pancakes that she began to cook at midnight and stored in the oven. When they left Al and Rosie Baglin took over. They had a jeep that Brooks had found abandoned on his Oxnard ranch. His gang, none of them mechanics, took it all apart, loaded it on a skiff, and reassembled it on the island. It ran, making the Baglins the most mobile of any island residents. Brooks continued to take an active part in the shearing operations and other necessary work projects. Then, in 1948, he was hit by a final blow. The Navy revoked his lease, giving him only 72 hours in which to remove all stock and improvements from the island.

It was a hopeless undertaking, but Brooks was forced to try to comply, as the Navy planned to place guided missile and bomb targets in the waters at the island's edge and on the island at Green Mountain. Upon arrival they discovered that Navy flyers had machine gunned both sheep and the pinnipeds indiscriminately. Rotting flesh fouled the air. Desperately, Brooks's men covered the island on foot and horseback, looking for sheep in the rugged ravines. But the time was too short. Over 500 sheep and four horses had to be left behind.[32]

Soon after this devastating experience, Brooks suffered a heart attack, and although he recovered he was never the same. In June, 1950 he got permission from the Navy to return briefly to San Miguel and remove more of his stock. Don Butler, his friend's son, took the roundup crew out this time and began work on the west end. The Navy had a lime circle around Green Mountain since they used it for target practice. After an initial misunderstanding over the six weeks allotted to Butler for the hunt, planes discontinued circling the target and the final collection of livestock began. But again, in the time allotted, every animal could not be found. Burros and sheep roamed the island throughout the 1950's, and as forage was ample for their reduced numbers, they thrived. Survival, however, was short-lived. Twice in the ensuing decade Navy personnel were sent out with orders to run them down and shoot them. Finally, after four days of aerial hunting in July, 1966, the slaughter was accomplished. Over a century of sheep grazing on San Miguel Island had come to an end.[33]

Meanwhile, the ranch complex so lovingly built by Waters, and nurtured by Brooks and Lester gradually fell into ruin. In 1967 it burned. For these men, as well as for George Nidever, sheep ranching on San Miguel island had meant more than a lucrative business enterprise. It had provided a deeply satisfying way of life: a sense of adventure, an identity and a challenge. William Waters and Herbert Lester proclaimed themselves kings of the island and carried the role far beyond the joking stage. Roberts Brooks found in it the romance and expression of masculinity on which he thrived. Today the site of their ranch house which had been so photographed and celebrated in its heyday, has been nominated for the

National Register of Historic Places, along with the old Nidever adobe as a part of the San Miguel Island Archaeological District. Thus will be provided a lasting tribute to a unique episode in the history of the island.

Chapter VIII

WORLD WAR II LOOKOUT STATION and MILITARY TESTING RANGE

Offshore Attacks and Downed Aircraft

Americans who did not live on the west coast at the outbreak of World War II would have a hard time understanding the fear and apprehension that took hold there following the attack on Pearl Harbor on December 7, 1941. That day had been a dazzling success for the Japanese. Southern California had poor coastal defenses, and the land adjacent to coastal ports was dotted with aircraft factories and oil fields. Californians knew this and most were stricken with a Great Fear. The Japanese were quick to launch attacks both on coastal shipping and on land targets, nothing to compare with Pearl Harbor, but still enough to cement a war-emergency mentality upon the region. On December 24, 1941 a Japanese submarine fired a torpedo at the freighter *Barbara Olson* near Point Vicente which juts out just north of the Los Angeles Harbor. The torpedo missed and exploded after passing the ship. Close by, the crew of the *S.S.Absaroka* and shore observers saw a Japanese submarine with a false fishing boat superstructure rise from the water and torpedo the *Absaroka* killing one seaman. Scores of people witnessed this attack, while others watched another slow moving submarine off Redondo Beach. On February 23, 1942 a submarine, seen by many people and by the police, shelled the Ellwood Oil Field on the coast north of Santa Barbara.[1]

The United States government ordered camouflage thrown over the shipyards and aircraft factories while citizens eagerly participated in blackout procedures. In areas close to the shore they taped black paper over their windows and at night drove on dark streets using at best their parking lights. Many of these night drivers were workers at the round-the-clock factories assigned to the swing and graveyard shifts.

The submarine attacks, anti-personnel bombs, and balloon attacks brought World War II to American soil, so the U.S. Navy set up a coastal lookout system with stations on each of the Channel Islands. San Miguel Island had been under Navy jurisdiction since 1934, and after the war was declared fell under the command of the Coastal Lookout Organization headquartered at the Eleventh Naval District in San Diego. The earliest wartime reference to the San Miguel Island Station was on December 13, 1941 when the weather observer on the island, Ranch Manager Lester, was informed that effective that date a temporary radio call had been assigned: Naval Lookout Station, San Miguel Island-292. However, by the end of December "Naval" was replaced with the word "Coastal" which was then used throughout the war. The Coastal Lookout Stations (CLS) were manned by Coast Guard, Army, and Navy personnel, and when fully manned each station had a staff of seven men to cover the twenty-four hour duty.[2]

A Navy patrol boat brought out two navy men to San Miguel who the island lessee, Robert Brooks, agreed to billet at the ranch house. Using the top of the house for a lookout, they mounted their transmitter and scanned the sea with binoculars for enemy traffic. Among the offshore patrol boats was the *Hermes,* a Coast Guard cutter which had long patrolled the islands and served as free transportation for island dwellers. It shortly sank one Japanese submarine outside the San Pedro Harbor and unofficially claimed a second.[3] Visitors ceased to call at the island, and the coastal silencing of radio stations was so effective that the ranch manager's family had to tune in eastern stations to get news of the war.

A month after Pearl Harbor the officer in charge of the Stations, Commander H. O. Hill, arrived on San Miguel Island aboard a seventeen-foot surf boat. The treacherous landing at Cuyler Harbor convinced Hill that all provisioning of the island would have to be done during

Betsy Lester Roberti

World War II, May 1942, the Lesters, Pomo their dog, and two Navy men at the Lookout Station.

the summer months. When Hill returned to San Diego he reported that the island had a smooth, well-marked airplane landing field about 1800 feet long with a standard wind sock. Because of the forceful winds, airplanes of a fairly large size could land there.[4] A dry lake near the western end of the island has also served as a landing field. Like everybody else Hill was impressed with Herbert Lester, a man he described as "distinctly of a high type of intelligence."[5]

Hill decided to have a wooden lookout tower built on San Miguel Peak, 831 feet high, and the Navy soon bulldozed a road from the ranch house to the tower and on to Point Bennett. Service men named it the Road to Mandalay. Seven of the eight Channel Islands had one Lookout; San Clemente being the farthest seaward had three, but none of the men had hand guns. Fear of unexpected attack subsided after the Battle of Midway in June of 1942, often considered the turning point of the war in the Pacific. The Lookout Stations were improved up to that date, then simply maintained. Service personnel worked on San Miguel till the lookout system was abolished July 1, 1945, a month prior to our dropping the bomb on Hiroshima.

The war years on San Miguel were so quiet that one military researcher observed that he could not think of a worse fate for an historian than to have his professional career hang on writing the war history of the Channel Islands. Walking the trails at sundown makes one think back upon the young men who daily mounted the tower on San Miguel Hill. Did they enjoy their safe assignment or fight off a biding loneliness as the day ended and they walked back to the ranch house and the mice.

The war did touch San Miguel one day in 1943 when a B-24 bomber flew into the north side of Green Mountain.[6] Events leading up to the crash began on July 4, 1943 when a B-24 based at Salinas Army Air Force Base and returning

Channel Islands National Park

A B-24 bomber flying blind on a heading for Point Conception struck Green Mountain in 1943.

from a long range overwater navigation mission ran low on fuel. Near the coastline of Santa Barbara the crew of ten bailed out. The aircraft crashed near the Cameusa Peak Forest Lookout ten miles inland from Santa Barbara at 2:00 a.m. On July 5 another B-24, and the one which would crash on San Miguel Island, was ordered out to search for the missing crew members. This B-24 carried twelve crew members, and its flight plan was to take headings for Bakersfield, Santa Barbara, Point Conception, and then to Salinas where it would land. It reported over Santa Barbara at 8:00 a.m., then there was radio silence.

On that morning Santa Barbara and the coast west of the city had low clouds, a ceiling of 300 to 500 feet, and cloud tops with clear vision above at 1600 feet. The B-24 had no radar. Apparently the plane was descending through the clouds with a heading on Point Conception. At about 500 feet it struck the rising slope of Green Mountain which peaked at 817 feet. The plane disintegrated. The Air Force made a search but found no signs of the B-24. Meanwhile, search parties picked up and saved eight of the ten crew members of the first B-24.

Robert Brooks, out tending sheep on March 19, 1944 discovered the wreckage. He walked back to the ranch house, reported it to Navy personnel there and led them to the scene. Brooks was appalled to see the Navy boys taking personal effects from the bodies of the crew members and commanded them to stop and to leave those things for the families of the deceased.

The Navy removed the remains of the crew, and filed a wreck report. See Appendix for further details. Brooks surveyed the landscape and out of curiosity climbed up on the Lookout Tower. From it the wreck was clearly visible but had remained undetected for almost a year. Piece by

Bill Roberts

Ranger Maki discovered this Blue Whistler fin at the former Island Bombing Range.

piece, the smaller memorabilia from the plane were taken off the B-24 and carried away by servicemen and sheep crewman alike. Some sizeable parts are still there on Green Mountain to mark the site of the crash.

Ironically, the incident was yet to bring about two more deaths. This happened when the wreckage was rediscovered in 1954. Hikers came upon what appeared to be human bones on Green Mountain, saw airplane parts, and assumed the wreck had never been reported. They returned to the mainland, and a quick military records check produced no crash report on San Miguel. The Coast Guard immediately sent out a boat, it struck the sailboat, *Aloha*, off Point Mugu and sank it, drowning two of the passengers. Shortly afterwards investigators uncovered the original crash record and brought the whole matter to an end.

Military Testing: Post World War II

The three years after July 1945 when the Coastal Lookout Stations were abolished were uneventful, and Robert Brooks continued to employ managers and to graze his sheep on San Miguel under a Navy lease. Then, in July, 1948 he was given seventy-two hours to remove his sheep and other property from the island. Leading up to military use of the island, a San Miguel Island Bombing Range Danger Area appeared in a Coast Guard Notice to Mariners in December. After this squadrons from March Field near Riverside, Castle Air Force Base at Merced, and from the Naval Air Station at Moffet Field began to compete for one-week practice slots. Each facility would have preferred uninterrupted use as the island was perfect for their exercises. Attack aircraft and fighter-bombers found it useful for exercises requiring a radar tracking site and dropped an inert bomb called the Blue Whistler. This was dropped at about a thousand feet and had a fin at the back which made a whistling sound. The round blue casing was filled with sand, and the five-pound powder charge made a puff and a mark when it impacted. Targets were offshore, but on a miss the Blue Whistler could strike the terrain and ruin some of the island's vegetation.[7]

Both Moffett Field and Castle Air Force Base found San Miguel entirely satisfactory for squadrons which required use of a high altitude target. To fulfill curriculum needs their flyers dropped 4,000 pound light-case bombs at altitudes up to and including 30,000 feet. As these exercises continued on into the 1950's and early 1960's, shrapnel and bomb casings were strewn all over the island. The Notice to Mariners about the new bombing range failed to keep fishing boats and other surface craft out of the area, and especially out of Cuyler Harbor. The squadrons dropped red flares and message blocks close to the boats and made low passes with bomb bays open, but the signals were not understood by the boatmen. Some planes circled Cuyler Harbor for over an hour before they could clear the area of pleasure craft. The nuisance was costly, so the Coast Guard made it a Permanent Danger Area and posted signs around the island. To make matters worse for the military, the San Miguel Island bombing range was closed from June 16, 1950 to July 9, 1950 so Robert Brooks could come out and try once again to remove his remaining livestock. Then, while the range was closed, the Korean War broke out placing the bombing range in even greater demand. Carrier-based squadrons from North Island, San Diego now stepped in and demanded priority use.[8]

In 1961 the Navy refused to submit San Miguel Island to a plan then being drafted for several of the islands by the National Park Service. It explained that the Pacific Missile Range facility at Point Mugu was launching missiles into polar orbit and that their flight paths went directly over the island. The entire island could be subject to impact by missile pieces if destructive action occurred

Mike Maki

Crater at Crook Point. Bullpup missiles were targeted for places distant from the pinnipeds and major archaeological sites.

during launch. No one could be on the island during southerly launchings and those launchings were rapidly increasing in number.[9] In 1963 San Miguel was placed under command of the Pacific Missile Range. The Navy agreed to a joint protection plan for natural and historic values with the Department of the Interior, but it held onto its priority for military use.[10]

The Pacific Missile Range employed the island in several advanced tests. In 1964 it began some land mass background studies to test radar guidance systems. The missile was launched southerly over the island from a boat to see how the radar guidance responded to land clutter. At that time we needed to know if we had a problem with the Russian Komar submarine. Could the Komar run in near an island, the radar on our missile lose the Komar, and the Komar then try to hit the island? After those tests the radar system was improved so that it locked onto the moving target, and the land mass in the background would not cause it to break lock. San Miguel's location was unique for those launches as well as for exercises to see if a missile could distinguish between the land and the target and for testing airborne systems. In the last the Pacific Missile Range wanted to know if San Miguel's land mass would confuse the missile electronic systems and the radar of a plane pursuing another aircraft over ocean and then over land.[11]

While these tests proceeded, Los Angeles Channel 13 KCOP-TV carried a program on May 3, 1965, "The Secret of San Miguel," and by its nature it encouraged people to go out to the island and search for buried treasure. The Navy hurriedly issued a public announcement warning that unexploded ordnance could be on the island and in the days afterward made a sweep for bombs over the whole surface of the island. However, due to the continuous high winds and shifting sand no one could know how successful the decontamination work had been. The next month Bullpup missile tests began at San Miguel with firings aimed at a barge anchored in Cuyler Harbor and followed up with land targets which the Range headquarters claimed were at a safe distance from archaeological and zoological sites. The island was also perfect as a tactical target area for fleet training. Planes could approach the target area from any direction at zero to a 20,000 foot altitude using various attack modes and employing both inert and live warheads.[12]

In order to avoid archaeological sites when setting up targets for tactical bombing missions, the Navy flew Charles Rozaire and George Kritzman of the Los Angeles Museum of Natural History out to the island in August of 1965 to map archaeological sites. Rozaire measured and made diagrams of the Ranch House and the old adobe while he was there. He wrote that the Navy barracks used during the war had been shot up by vandals and a tally kept on the door of all the island foxes the pleasure seekers had killed.[13]

The Navy eventually got tired of small boat owners who would not heed notices to stay out of San Miguel waters and of vandals who came onto the island, tore down metal signs bolted to steel posts, shot up the buildings, and used the seals for target practice. It was not the general public, but, as one official put it, a small cantankerous group. Over a huge outcry by fishermen, abalone hunters, the Sierra Club, Western Oil and Gas, and various yacht clubs the Navy established a Danger Zone closed to all during firing but open to general navigation at other times. The zone included the east end of the island plus a three-mile wide offshore area on all sides contiguous to the land zone. It included Cuyler Harbor. Landing or going ashore was prohibited without permission of the Pacific Missile Range.[14]

Areas such as San Nicolas and San Clemente Islands and several desert areas were available for missile testing and practice firing, but only San Miguel offered the realism needed for pilot training. Situated at the westerly end of the island chain, it presented a minimum safety hazard while offering maximum security. Commander Sharp at the Pacific Missile Range claimed, "No other target areas in the United States allow for attack by two or more aircraft at once, or permit pilots to determine their own altitude, range, angle, and release position...In final substance, it is the last such area left."[15] In 1966 proficiency training on the island included the Bullpup missile, the folding fin aircraft rocket, bombs, the ZUNI Missile, 20mm cannon weapons, NIKE targets, simulated truck convoys, and tanks. Plans were underway to build bridge targets and to create land targets for the fleet.

For some reason, during the 1970's military use of the island wound down, and in 1975 the Navy signed an agreement with the Department of the Interior allowing the National Parks Service some administrative latitude over natural resources on San Miguel. In late 1976 the only Pacific Missile Test Center asset on the island itself was an automatic weather station. A target barge was, however, anchored a mile or so south of the Island's eastern tip for target practice.[16] The danger zone surrounding the eastern end of the island still prevailed. Squadrons came from Miramar, North Island, Lemoore, Moffet Field, and other bases for practice. Training manuals that year specified that live ordnance could be used only on San Clemente Island, so strikes at the target southeast of San Miguel were made with inert ordnance such as a small Blue Whistler.[17] Military exercises still continue there several times a week using the island's land mass. San Miguel's unique location will keep it valuable in the eyes of the Navy for many years to come.

Chapter IX

NATIONAL PARK MANAGEMENT

Lighthouse Bureau to National Monument Management

San Miguel Island passed through several government agencies before it was proclaimed a part of the Channel Islands National Park. After the United States acquired it from Mexico in the mid-nineteenth century, Congress assigned it to the Lighthouse Bureau then administered by the Fifth Auditor of the United States Treasury, but San Miguel received no attention from that quarter. The Department of Treasury created a separate Lighthouse Board in 1852, California falling under the Twelfth District, and there too the Board's archives are devoid of any mention of San Miguel until 1896. Two incidents bear responsibility for this attention. The first was a newspaper article published in 1895 reporting that England could legally take San Miguel for a coaling station since the island had never been specifically mentioned in the 1848 treaty between Mexico and the United States. The second event was a dramatic slump slide in Cuyler Harbor in March of 1895. In response to the English menace, President Grover Cleveland sent out Marshall Nicholas Covarrubias and some surveyors in July, 1896, and the sovereignty issue disappeared. The Department of Commerce took over the Lighthouse Bureau in 1903, just as the American public was becoming aware of conservation.

Helped along by the Progressive Movement and led by President Theodore Roosevelt the conservationists clamored for a bill in Congress that would give the president the power to set aside areas of scientific and scenic value. The Antiquities Act of 1906 did this and forbade disturbance of ruins and archaeological remains on federal land without the permission of the responsible land management agency. But the Department of the Interior people wanted more, wanted it to mandate protection of properties for natural phenomena as well. President Theodore

Roosevelt, with his great flair for publicity, backed the idea in his 1907 annual message to congress and in 1909 forty-one state conservation commissions were established. Millions of Americans were caught up in the idea by 1913, and that year several letters came to the Department of Commerce protesting the overgrazing at San Miguel Island. However, the Lighthouse Bureau had signed its first legal grazing lease in 1911 and was satisfied with its tenants. Instead of cutting back on the number of sheep, Bureau Chief Rhodes defended the grazing industry for its contribution to the public good, and left the nearly 4,000 sheep on San Miguel to forage. Passed over by the nation's first conservation efforts, the island, Richardson Rock, and Prince Island were made official lighthouse reservations in 1917. For the ensuing two decades little paperwork entered their files except for grazing leases.[1] In 1916 Congress created the National Park Service.

Franklin Roosevelt transferred San Miguel Island and Prince Island from the Commerce Department to the Secretary of the Navy in 1934. The Navy picked up the current grazing lease, but bending to public pressure put a limit upon the number of sheep. Flocks that had exceeded 6,000 in the 1860s and 4,000 at the turn of the century were cut back to a maximum 1,200 in 1938 and later to 1,000. These were the first moves by the government to conserve the island's rare resources.[2] Meanwhile, Congress advised the Lighthouse Bureau to save several of its offshore California islands for Park use. Bureau Chief Rhodes suggested releasing Santa Barbara Island and Anacapa Island in 1932, but the National Park Service did not have a chance to come out and look at the islands. Perhaps for this reason it suggested to Rhodes that he ask Congress to give these two islands to the State of California for a park. Rhodes ignored the idea, and in 1937 he again appealed to the National Park Service giving them detailed descriptions of land available for transfer at the California islands. Park Service Assistant Director, Dr. H. C. Bryant, finally came out from Washington D. C., made a boat trip around the islands, and landed on big, privately owned Santa Cruz

Island. He saw the government-owned islands only through field glasses, and since it was September they looked brown, desolate, and entirely uninviting. Bryant didn't see anything spectacular about the plants on the larger Santa Rosa and Santa Cruz Islands either and commented that plants on them could be of value but only because of the limited range that they occupied in the world. As for the government-owned islands, he wrote that they were barren of rare species and covered only with grass, annuals, or coast live oak.[3] San Miguel did not even support a live oak.

The man who apparently turned things around was Theodore D. S. Cockerell, a biologist from the University of Colorado. He had been collecting specimens on the islands and gathering data from other scientists for years. After an expedition to San Miguel, Santa Barbara, and Anacapa Islands in 1937 he wrote an article about the extraordinary importance of the islands for natural history studies and got his work into the hands of the right people. Although the chain of events is not clear, Cockerell's role in educating the Washington office of the National Park Service cannot be underestimated. The next year, 1938, President Franklin D. Roosevelt created the Channel Islands National Monument which included all of Santa Barbara Island and Anacapa Island except for small areas reserved for lighthouse use. Newton Drury, Director of the Park Service, then requested a study of San Miguel Island. The Regional Biologist, Lowell Sumner, made a survey of the island and urged the Park Service to take immediate action to save its outstanding plant and wild life. His summary read in part:

> *...The present number of sheep (1100) would undoubtedly represent a conservative stocking under normal conditions, nature now is forcing man to pay the penalty for gross malpractice committed many years ago. For this reason, 1100 sheep now are destructive of the remnant of the island's resources, although originally such a number might have been pastured there indefinitely with little or no harm.*[4]

Had the Park Service in Washington taken immediate action and asked for San Miguel to be added to the Channel Islands National Monument, the Navy might have transferred San Miguel to the Monument in 1939. Neither happened. Superintendent E.T. Scoyen administered the two monument Islands, Santa Barbara Island and Anacapa Island, from his base at the Sequoia National Park. He had no equipment such as boats or places to house boats or any Sequoia personnel free to work on the islands. Biologist Sumner spent some time on Santa Barbara and Anacapa Islands drawing up a management plan, and teams of local scientists from the Los Angeles Museum of Natural History and from the Santa Barbara Botanical Gardens made field trips to the Monument and San Miguel. In May of 1941 Superintendent Scoyen set out for a first-hand inspection. He probably saw the islands covered with new spring grasses and spotted with bright yellow coreopsis and witnessed the usual display of elephant seals and the other pinnipeds. He wrote to the National Park Service Director that he had never spent such an interesting day from the wildlife standpoint in his life and added, "Boy! We've got something out there in the Channel Islands."[5] In August, 1941 Sequoia had a new Superintendent, John R. White. The main wildlife attraction for him was not on the Monument Islands but on the west end of San Miguel where he saw thousands of sea lions and sea elephants and even touched one. White requested protection for the waters adjoining the Monument Islands where the seals and sea lions were a nuisance to fishermen, were fired upon, and were thus in the most danger. He had been told that just about every fisherman had a gun on his boat for that purpose. The boundary for the Monument was at the high water mark which made National Park protection very difficult.

Following the Scoyen and White recommendations and in November, 1941 the Park Service told the Navy that San Miguel Island should have monument status. A few weeks later on December 7 the Japanese bombed Pearl Harbor. When the Navy was able to answer, it replied that the island was already protected and that any transfer in status at that time was foolish to discuss. During World War II no one from Sequoia Park visited the Monument. Happily, wartime restrictions against private boats kept away the poachers and seal shooters.

After the war Thomas Vint, Chief Landscape Architect for the Park Service, evaluated the islands for possible national park development but personally judged them lacking in scenic beauty. On the other hand he found the ocean life spectacular and the underwater world a big show. Thanks to Vint's lobbying, President Harry Truman signed a proclamation in February, 1949 extending Park Service jurisdiction one nautical mile beyond the shores of the two Monument islands. Even though San Miguel was not in any way part of the Monument, the inquiries regarding management of offshore resources usually prompted some advice about San Miguel's waters as well. For example, a botanist at the University of California, Berkeley, W. A. Setchell, was asked for an opinion and he advised that the giant kelps of the Pacific coast had no counterparts elsewhere in the Northern Hemisphere. He wanted the kelp beds at San Miguel graded and mapped. While Anacapa had thin beds, San Miguel had very heavy beds grading down to thin. Such areas, he urged, should be converted into a national monument and preserved.

Between 1939 and 1957 no National Park representative landed on San Miguel. Lowell Sumner made an air inspection of the northern Channel Islands in 1948, recommended monument status for San Miguel, but got no encouragement. When he conferred with regional specialists about a seashore survey of San Miguel in 1957, he again urged protection arguing that San Miguel was approximately fourteen times as large as Santa Barbara Island and had a correspondingly greater wealth of unique biological features. He reminded the Park Service that it was the federal government that had permitted the destruction of San Miguel through continual grazing;

consequently, it was up to the government to restore the land. At last his superiors listened, and a few days after receiving Sumner's recommendation the Regional Director wrote to his superiors asking that San Miguel Island be added to the Channel Islands National Monument, but it was not. In July, 1957 the Monument headquarters was moved from the Sequoia and Kings Canyon National Parks to the Cabrillo National Monument headquarters in San Diego. Superintendent Donald A. Robinson recruited an historian, Francis Holland, for the combined monuments. Holland, produced a *History of San Miguel Island* in 1961.

San Miguel's exclusion from national park management was not an isolated case. For fifteen years national emergencies had held back improvements at the national parks all over the country. While visitors doubled, staffing fell behind. Magazine articles such as Bernard De Voto's "Let's Close the National Parks" in *Harpers* drew a clear picture for the public. Out of the uproar came a National Park Service ten-year plan, Mission 66 [1966]. The Channel Islands National Monument's book-length contribution set down the geological, biological and historical values of the monument for the planners to see, drawing attention to the existing monument islands and to the potential at San Miguel.

Further emphasis on Monument expansion came in February 1961 when President John F. Kennedy sent a special message to Congress about the national parks imploring, "America's health, morale, and culture have long benefited from our national parks and forests but they are not now adequate to meet the needs of a fast-growing and more mobile population."[6] He asked Secretary of the Interior Stewart Udall to conduct a survey to determine where additional seashore parks should be proposed. The Santa Barbara *News Press* printed the story, and Editor Thomas Storke and other California backers petitioned for the Channel Islands to be a national park. Thomas Storke urged the two California Senators Kuchel and Engle to lead the way and opened correspondence with an old friend of his, James K. Carr, Undersecretary of the Interior.

Storke's proposed park would include Santa Barbara, Anacapa, Santa Cruz, Santa Rosa, and San Miguel Islands.

Undersecretary Carr was so enthusiastic that he put forth a "Days of the Dons" idea which would make the Park a living museum. No automobiles, no motorcycles and only cattle and sheep would roam the island hills. In the coves would be replicas of the galleons and caravels of Cabrillo's day. Tourist accommodations would be authentic reproductions of the *posadas*: adobe walls, red tile roofs, and patio gardens. Park personnel would dress as Dons and carry guitars. The idea appealed to Ed Stanton, part owner of Santa Cruz, who at one time had responded to a park idea with, "I don't want all the bums running wild on my island and a park would mean just that!"[7] Conrad Wirth, Director of the National Park Service, made plans to come out to Santa Barbara in May, 1961 while Storke dined with the Chandlers, publishers of the *Los Angeles Times* , to educate them. Storke then reminded his old friend Chief Justice Warren of a hunt they had made together on Santa Rosa Island. Both Stanton and Ed Vail, the latter a part owner of Santa Rosa, favored the sale of their lands to the Park Service in May of 1961. Storke explained to James Carr that the project should move quickly since property values moved upward so rapidly that in five years the Park Service might not be able to come up with the money. The plan did not move quickly. California already had one bill pending in congress on a Point Reyes National Seashore proposal, and the possibility of getting two bills through in one session was remote.

Meanwhile, the Navy admitted that it had no preservation experience, but it had to keep San Miguel. So, it got together with Park personnel in 1962 and drew up some interim agreements for the park service to aid in management of the island. The environmentalists were already complaining to the Navy for conditions on San Clemente and San Nicholas Islands, and the Navy had pointed out that it had no funds, little transportation, and limited personnel. Near San Miguel it needed to launch missiles and for that it had to close down the island now and then. The following year the Departments of Navy and of Interior signed an accord for "Protection of Natural Values and Historic and Scientific Objects on San Miguel and Prince Islands." Accordingly, the National Park Service would take inventory and promote recovery or reintroduction of rare and locally extinct plants and animals. It would in all ways cooperate with the Navy in its rules and management of the islands as both departments recognized priority for military use.

Joint Venture: Navy and National Park

The Channel Islands National Monument headquarters moved into temporary quarters in Oxnard in 1967, thus becoming independent of the Cabrillo Monument. Superintendent William H. Ehorn who would head the Channel Islands National Park arrived in June of 1974 and provided excellent leadership for the crucial fifteen years that lay ahead. One of his first tasks was to comply with an amendment to the National Park agreement with the Navy

Channel Islands National Park

Park Headquarters in Nidever Canyon, 1990.

allowing the National Park Service to spend funds on San Miguel Island, to enforce Park Service regulations, and to develop a tightly controlled visitor program. Specialists in geology, biology, history, and archaeology went to work on reports detailing the natural resources of San Miguel. A temporary ranger, Mike Hill, set up a tent in the arroyo south of Cuyler Harbor and began to escort visitors out and along the long Road to Mandalay leading to Point Bennett. In 1977 Ehorn had a Statement for Management ready as well as an agreement with the National Marine Fisheries Service to manage and protect the pinnipeds that were fast returning to the island.

Meanwhile, Californians led by Editor Storke pressured for the Channel Islands National Park idea. In 1963 Senator Claire Engle backed a bill for a Channel Islands National Seashore, seashore rather than park since in this way the government would not need to acquire all of the private property on Santa Cruz and Santa Rosa Islands. No action was taken. Then Carr retired and Engle died. In 1966 five bills came before the House on the matter, two before the Senate. Momentum slowed during the 1970's, but the bill for a park did pass in March, 1980. It was all that Editor Storke had asked for: the five islands and Prince Island in Cuyler Harbor specified as well. The law authorized funds with which to buy the private lands on the larger islands. San Miguel Island had always been government land and came into the Park as such, however with reservations made for use and ultimate jurisdiction by the Department of the Navy. The National Park Service did not have management authority for marine life below the low tide zone and thus could not protect it. Fortunately, this same year, 1980, all waters within six miles of the five islands were designated national marine sanctuaries. This insured protection of the complete marine environment around San Miguel including the incomparable kelp beds and the myriad sea life dependent upon them. The Channel Islands National Marine Sanctuary headquartered in the City of Santa Barbara coordinates with the National Oceanic and Atmospheric Administration and the California Department of Fish and Game as well as with the Park Service in protecting marine resources and in controlling and providing for the water's use by recreational divers, boating enthusiasts, and people who come out simply to view the extraordinary nature of San Miguel. Some ideas about how to get out to the island and what awaits the viewer lie ahead.

Monitoring the Island's Ecosystems

Every national park is a treasure, and most offer beauty and a retreat from the stresses of modern, urban life. Factor in isolation from the mainland to reach the essence of the Channel Islands National Park. Isolation has provided the opportunity for the evolution of distinct taxa and an "American Galapagos" a few miles from the City of Santa Barbara. San Miguel's pronounced isolation as the westernmost island of the chain has made it a reservoir of wild genetic material that is found nowhere else in the world. Sea birds and marine mammals in particular, species that once bred in many areas of the mainland coast, can only be found there. Both the chapter on pinnipeds earlier in this book and the chapter to be seen ahead about the flora and fauna of the island treat with these taxa. These ecosystems of terrestrial and marine species are under constant inventory and now receive long-term protection and monitoring.

Monitoring the ecosystems has revealed standard vital signs. Such standards are likened to ecological "miners' canaries." But we must watch the canaries or their warnings will be lost. Restoration and preservation of the island's ecosystems took a great leap forward when it fell under the National Park System. Monitoring provided regular assessments of ecosystem health and determined the limits of natural variation from normal conditions. Now, when variation exceeds those limits, the biologists put their heads together to see what can be done. Since not all species could be monitored, the specialists selected broadly from different levels of life forms, selected species

Dana Seagar

U.S. Fish and Wildlife mammalogist tagging a seal.

with endangered status, looked at harvested taxa such as marine resources, and watched popular "heroic" species such as the Island Fox.

A major indicator of ecosystem health is the way in which populations change. Contributing to the change is phenology, a study of the relationship between climate and periodic biological phenomena such as migration and breeding. The El Nino effect upon kelp beds was noted, and weather conditions are monitored continually.

Park rangers serve as emergency medical technicians for the island's ecosystems. They identify overt threats to the systems and protect ailing ecosystems until long-term treatment can be brought about. The ranger at San Miguel is presently bringing out volunteer weed pullers to root out an exotic species from the mainland that is impacting the ancient and rare island ecosystem. Rangers take a daily census of visitors, study patterns of visitation and visitor impact upon the ecosystems. All of this is a part of "watching the canary."

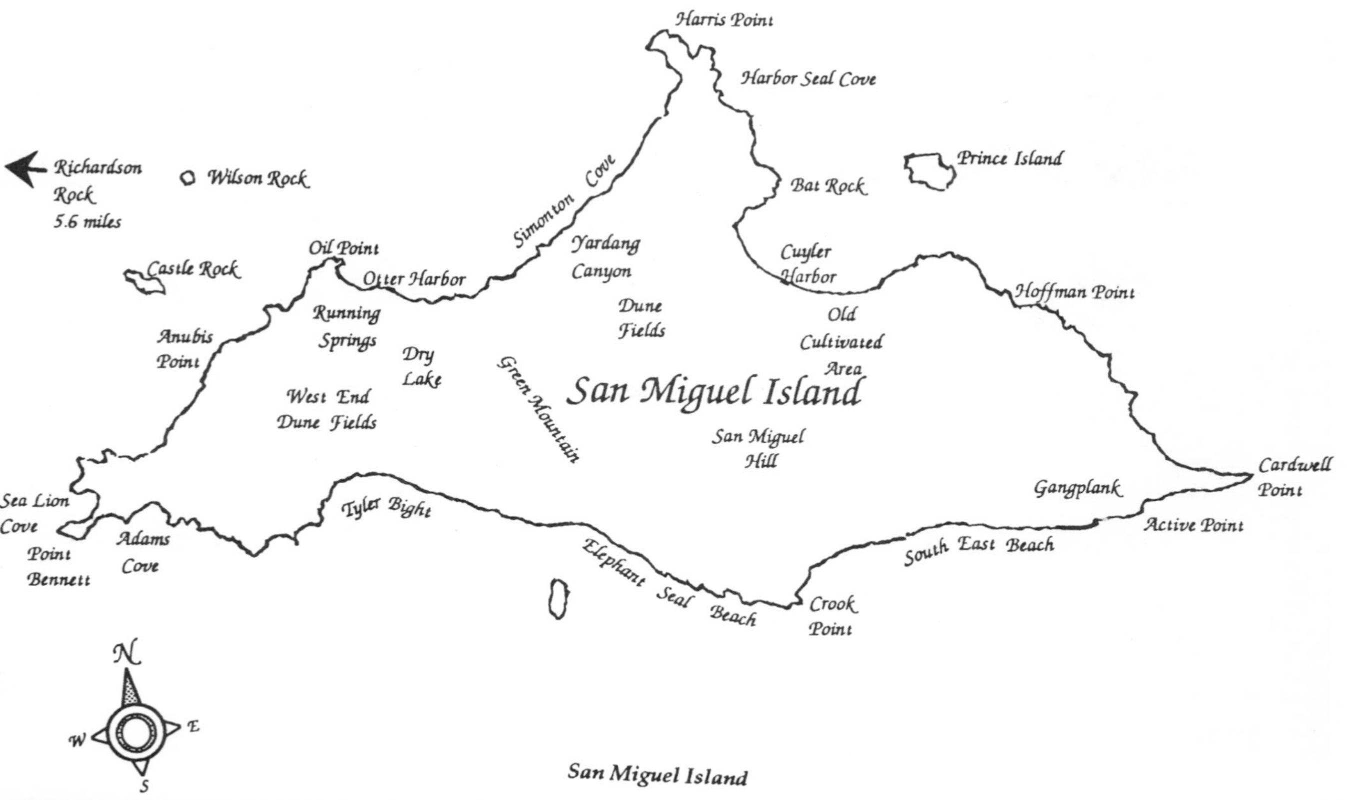

San Miguel Island

Chapter X

EXCURSIONS TO SAN MIGUEL ISLAND

Introduction

One of the ultimate Channel Islands experiences is to explore the waters around San Miguel Island; then to walk up Nidever Canyon on the island's north side, stand on the plateau above, and look back at the sea. The sea around is teaming with marine life supported by the upwelling of rich nutrients and by kelp beds. These elements shaped the evolution of sea life here thousands of years ago. Hiking up to this plateau, you will travel through a historical record of geologic time dating back to the Pleistocene. Look carefully, as it is written into old beach terraces and stored in the sides of the cliffs. Aware of these historic beginnings and San Miguel's long isolation from the landmass of coastal California, the visitor is prepared to witness a world profoundly different from the mainland.

The island is protected by national park status and the waters surrounding it by their designation as a National Marine Sanctuary. Priceless natural, cultural, and historical features are thus being protected against the everpresent tendencies of man to change, exploit, and tame. Among them are over 500 relatively undisturbed archaeological sites. Through careful management, the island's wilderness character will be preserved for present and future generations to enjoy and to learn from.

Because of its isolation and difficulty of access, San Miguel is one of the least-visited areas of our national park system. The Park Service in cooperation with the U.S. Navy has gradually opened the island to public visitation: first by ranger-led hikes in the late seventies, then in 1988 overnight camping was permitted for the first time.

The Passage

Air travel to San Miguel Island is altogether feasible since a small airstrip and a dry lake afford landings.

However, the Park Service wisely and rigorously restricts landings to the needs of administrative personnel. The essence of the island lies in its back-to-nature wilderness, and for those lucky enough to go there it serves as a window to an earlier, uncorrupted period, an era served at best by boats.

Throughout recorded history man has come to the island by boat: the Indian in his plank canoe or *tomol,* the Spanish in their galleons, the otter hunters and others in big sailing vessels and steamships. Visitors travel to the island by small craft, so in this way the San Miguel Island adventure begins the minute they step aboard. As the boat makes its way out of the harbor and into the waters of the Santa Barbara Channel you lose the urban connection and very quickly sense getting away from all the pressures of our electronic and auto oriented society. The overwhelming sea environment turns your dependence upon the boat, upon navigation and weather, and upon sea conditions. Sealife surrounds you as you sense the mainland receding and see the outlines of the easterly Channel Islands, Anacapa, Santa Cruz, and Santa Rosa, pass before you. Hours before your arrival you feel the relationship that everything on San Miguel Island has with the sea.

The Park Service has a concessionaire service for boat travel, Island Packers, Inc., based in Ventura alongside the Channel Islands National Park Headquarters on Spinnaker Drive. This service offers both two-day excursion trips on their large boats with sleeper accommodations and camper tranportation to and from the island. All departures are dependent upon sea conditions. The company publishes new excursion schedules annually. The Santa Barbara Museum of Natural History organizes trips on a well-equipped boat which provides sleeping and dining facilities. Both a museum naturalist and a park ranger accompany the group on island hikes. Boats leaving from Santa Barbara Harbor need three hours to complete the trip out. Private charter boats and fishing excursion boats are also available.

San Miguel's sometimes rough and chilly waters are not

for everyone. Only vessels under the command of experienced skippers and capable of withstanding severe weather are advised to make the passage. Those intending to go by private boat can find the information they will need in Brian M. Fagan, *Cruising Guide to California's Channel Islands*. This, along with nautical chart 18727 should keep you out of foul anchorage, off rocks, free of kelp, and take you into a safe harbor on the island.

The kind of boat, of course, will determine the adventure in store for the passage out. Small fast boats traveling in good weather can make the trip in two hours or less. On the other hand a small sailing craft encountering changes in wind and current, fog conditions, or intense Pacific swells might have to put in at one of the anchorages on Santa Cruz or Santa Rosa Island and take several days to complete the trip. Robert Brooks, the island's longest lessee, once got as far as the island, but the fog was so dense he could only sense where he was by the sound of the waves slapping the shore. He waited at a safe distance for a week before he could see Cuyler Harbor and come in for a landing.

Whale watching, dolphin spotting, identifying coastal landmarks, sighting mountain peaks and landing spots on the other Channel Islands, and fishing are all part of the trip. On a good day the Channel makes for excellent cruising.

As you sail or motor past Santa Rosa Island and closer to San Miguel Island, the waters of the channel are no longer protected in the lee of Point Conception. The Point itself is considered one of the most treacherous areas for small craft along the California coast, but you will not be sailing that far. Winds coming from the north hit the land mass at full force and speed up as they are restricted in rounding the Point in a typical "venturi" effect. Winds at the cape can be fifty percent to one hundred thirty percent higher than strong offshore breezes. They are gusty, heighten the swells, and during storms the waves have reached heights of forty feet. However, this is very rare and a sturdy yacht can cruise this fascinating area in comfort.[1] As they bend around the land mass these same winds beat against San Miguel Island and into San Miguel Passage at the east end of the island. While these conditions underlie an exciting and even disastrous maritime history in these waters, your trip having been planned by an experienced captain should be a pleasant one.

Excursions on San Miguel Island

The National Park Service welcomes landing and day excursions on San Miguel Island the year around. Landing is permitted only at Cuyler Harbor, and should you anchor a private boat there you may take your small boat or skiff ashore and use the beach during the daytime. Landing on any other beach is prohibited to prevent adverse impacts on marine mammals. At this writing a permit from the National Park Service is needed to proceed further onto the island since the Park manages and protects it. This free permit allowing you day entry or a maximum of two nights camping may be obtained in advance of your visit from the park headquarters in Ventura. You may also take a chance upon obtaining a permit once there by contacting the Ranger via Marine Channel 16; but this affords no guarantee for island entry. Your chances will depend on what the ranger is doing that day. In the past the island has been used as a missile test range, and unexploded live ordnance is occasionally uncovered by the shifting sands. The United States Navy as partner of the Pacific Missile Test Range still has ultimate control and jurisdiction over the island, and their testing schedule takes precedence over all other uses. The Pacific Missile Test Range maintained a target in the waters southeast of the island for some years, but it is no longer there. Unexploded ordnance remains an important reason why a park ranger must accompany all visitors. Whether boating around the island or planning to land, you must heed the warnings on your nautical charts and on the current Local Notice to Mariners before entering the Naval Warning Zone on and around the east end of the island. Check with the Pacific

Missile Test Range at Point Mugu or with the United States Coast Guard on the day of your visit to find out if all is clear.

Contact the Island Ranger on VHF Marine Band Radio, Channel 16 between 7:00 and 8:00 p.m. the evening before, or between 7:00 and 8:00 a.m. the morning of your scheduled visit to arrange a meeting time and place. The maximum number of people allowed on the island each day is 30. Yours may not be the only group accompanying the Island Ranger the day you go ashore.

You often awaken to a calm but overcast morning; however, the summer sun usually comes out about midday. Landing on the beach may be a wet experience, so those who have done it advise taking extra dry clothes and to place cameras and other fragile items in plastic bags. The best place to land your dinghy is at the northwest corner of the bay by the large prominent palm trees. Note the rusty old iron stanchions that were driven into the rocks by Robert Brooks and his workers. They lead out into the water and mark the location of the sheep landing dock.[2] A park sign is located at this point and park information is available within a storage canister attached to this sign. A visitor register may be there too. The trail to the ranger station runs along the beach for approximately one half mile to a large canyon. A trail sign directs you up the canyon to the ranger station. It is a long row from the northwest corner of the bay to this section of the beach below Nidever Canyon, and there is a good possibility of being dunked, so an approach right at the canyon is not advised.

Cuyler Harbor has a broad, two-mile long beach of fine white sand. Behind it the high cliffs are draped with sand blown from the North Shore at Simonton Cove across and down. Cuyler is wonderful for walking, jogging and for beach combing. Intermittently, springs break out of the rocky cliffs sending rivulets into the surf. The nineteenth-century sheep ranchers picnicked on this beach, just as you will. If the water conditions are good, there is excellent kayaking and snorkeling. Fishing and shell collecting from the shore, however, are not permitted. And you can swim here too as did Mrs. Waters after a Sunday picnic in 1888.

If you have a permit to go further onto the island than the beach, the ranger will meet you and present you with options for exploring the island. The hiking is considered moderately strenuous; however distances can be long, especially when you are headed into the wind. Choose a hike that best matches your physical conditioning and time available. You will need to bring two quarts of water, and a lunch is suggested. The following is a list of possible day hikes with approximate one-way trail mileages from Cuyler Harbor and time equivalents. Remember, your group will only be able to go as far as the least physically fit person in the group.

Ranger Station	1.0 miles	.5 hours
Cabrillo Monument	1.4 miles	1.0 hours
Campground	1.5 miles	1.0 hours
San Miguel Hill	2.5 miles	1.5 hours
Caliche Forest	3.0 miles	2.0 hours
Point Bennett	8.0 miles	3.5 hours

Walks to Harris Point, Simonton Cove, and Cardwell Point can occasionally be arranged.[3]

The sixteen-mile round trip hike to Point Bennett begins early. Led by a Park Ranger who is also a naturalist, it will first take you up through Nidever Canyon past the ranger station. A separate trail leads away from the ranger station to the buried ruins of the old adobe, often called the Nidever adobe. The area is revegetating and jungle-like so that the ends of two or three exposed rafters are all you can see. Upon taking the main visitor's trail up to the plateau above Cuyler Harbor, the fresh air and sense of remoteness and solitude all strike at once. A monument erected to honor Juan Rodriguez Cabrillo stands on a northern promontory, and south of it the site of the large ranch complex built by William Waters and by the long-term lessee Robert Brooks. Ruins of a chimney and a cistern are all that remain of the structures today. After crossing the

Bill Roberts

Cuyler Harbor's two-mile beach.

narrow air strip originally laid out by George Hammond in the 1930's, the trail leads across the island to San Miguel Hill (elevation 831 feet). Debris of the World War II lookout tower remained for some time, and an automated weather station operates there today. The "Road to Mandalay," is a path leading to the extreme west end of the island. Walking along this you pass close to the spot where the B-24 bomber crashed into Green Mountain, see the dry lake where the Park Service lands small aircraft, the Caliche Forest, and finally come to the National Marine Fisheries Service Station above Point Bennett. Following the ranger's instructions, we may come reasonably close to the elephant seals and other pinnipeds during certain times of the year. This display in itself is ample reward for the trip, especially for the photographer. The spring months provide a spectacular wildflower show. The wind will be up by now, providing the freshest air in the world for the long hike back to Cuyler Harbor.

The walk to Cardwell Point at the extreme east end of

Bill Roberts

Tennis pro Betsy Lester Roberti (left) returned in 1979 to show the author the places where she had played.

the island takes the same heading as the air strip, progresses through old pastures, and follows the tire marks of a jeep road often used by Brooks and his ranch managers after 1947.[4] Waves crash upon Cardwell's wild and exciting shore from two directions forming a "V" where they collide. Decidedly, no surfing here. To the south and on the rocks at Active Point lies the remains of the broken steel hull of the USS *Tortuga.* Retracing the path west and looking to your right you can spot several wet *barrancas* that join to form Willow Canyon with its outlet to the beach between Challenge Point and Hoffman Point.

Hiking is not for all, but everyone can enjoy nature watching, resting, visiting, photography, and sensing why everyone loves this island. Visitors can roam within an approximately 80 acre area around the campground and, since only a few people are ever on the island, you may well find a moment when you alone can descend to Cuyler's beach. The harbor appears empty except for the birds perched upright on Judge Rock. Prince Island, a stately loaf

Bill Roberts

Hikers led by Ranger returning from Point Bennett.

spread across the entrance, is teaming with life that is invisible from shore. Feel the excitement of just being there. Sea birds and sea sounds are everywhere.

Camping

The camping experience on San Miguel is truly unique and will test your ability to adapt to the island's sometimes harsh surroundings. Strong winds and fog are the island constants in this back-to-nature experience. The small campground is located above Nidever Canyon, near the Ranch Historic Area and approximately 1.5 miles from Cuyler Harbor landing cove. An old fence line designates the ranch plot, and campers cannot wander outside of this from 7:00 p.m. until 7:00 a.m. The campsites are comprised of individual sites (1-6 people) and a group site (7-12) people. A pit toilet facility is provided, and basic wind shelters are installed at each campsite location. The Island Packers at Ventura offer transportation to the island for campers.

Since you may need specialized equipment to adapt to the elements, it is suggested that you bring a strong tent, a sleeping bag, and warm, waterproof clothes. Other required supplies include water, a campstove, and a first aid kit. The campsites can be reserved at the park headquarters in Ventura. All campsite reservations are subject to a first come, first serve basis. A maximum of 30 campers is allowed. There are no fees. Memorial Day may signal the opening, and November 1st the closing. Camping dates are subject to the availability of the Island Ranger.

Excursions Around San Miguel Island

As will be recalled, San Miguel Island was proclaimed a part of the Channel Islands National Park in 1980. The same year the six miles of submerged land and ocean surrounding the island was designated part of the Channel Islands National Marine Sanctuary. Sport and fishing regulations are set by the California Department of Fish and Game, while the Sanctuary sees to the ecological wellbeing of the area. One should take note that boating is normally permitted on all sides of the island except west of a line drawn between Judith Rock on the southwest and Castle Rock on the northwest. In this area, boats are prohibited closer than 300 yards to the shore. This rule is enforced to protect the pinniped rookeries on the west end of the island, Point Bennett. Overnight anchorages are limited to Cuyler Harbor and Tyler Bight. Further, boats traveling within 300 yards of the shoreline, where permitted, or in the anchorages, must proceed quietly while not exceeding a speed of five miles per hour. No person except those with official duties may climb onto the offshore islands and rocks which lie in the Sanctuary due to the presence of extremely sensitive sea-bird colonies, especially on Prince Island. Over ninety percent of the watery zone around the island is open to visitors, a boating area. Here one may snorkel, skin dive, scuba dive, photograph and fish. Sportfishers do cast their lines in

Dan Gotshall

Scuba divers love the fantastic variety of marine life.

these water, and the take is outstanding. However, as Ranger Rob Danno observed:

> *The whole of the California Coast is open to fishing. Maybe within the boundaries of this National Park and Marine Sanctuary people could come to just marvel at the beauty that abounds in this environment, to accept it, and to respect its right to exist undisturbed.*

One of the special things about San Miguel waters is that you can get on a boat in the warm Southern California waters and in one day be in waters matching those off the northern and central California coast. The northern California system of marine life seen here is about the same as you would see in places like Monterey Bay. The island lies in the Oregonean, cold water province. For example, the Garibaldi *Hypsypops rubicundus* are usually last seen at South Point on Santa Rosa Island. The California Sheephead *Semicossyphus pulcher* are seen, because San Miguel is near the northern end of their range as are the warm water Kelp Bass *Paralabrax clathratus*. In this Oregonean, cold water province you will see Cabazon *Scorpaenichthys marmoratus*, Olive Rockfish *Sebastes serranoides* and many other rockfishes.[5]

The persistent upwelling of cold waters off Point Conception constantly renews a food chain that supports both animal and plant life. The kelp beds around the Channel Islands, and specifically at San Miguel, probably have no counterparts in the western hemisphere. Anchored to the rocky ocean bottom, they have no root system to get sustenance out of the ground. Instead they take phosphorus and nitrogen out of the nutrient rich waters here. In turn, the kelp serve as food to a long chain of marine life, a unique kelp-bed community. Although Hawaii's warm waters and colorful fish are popular, the nutrient balance there is less supportive. These cold waters with kelp forests offer far more diversity in that algae, invertebrates, and fish all abound.[6]

The kelp beds mapped in the past at Point Bennett, on the south side of the island, and at the eastern extremity of Cuyler Harbor have undergone change. Kelp forests are dynamic, they come and go. El Nino of 1982-1983 brought in a rush of warm water lacking in nutrients, and most of the kelp at San Miguel disappeared. Recovery has been patchy. Kelp does not have the persistence of a pine forest! The kelp canopy in Cuyler Harbor had still not reappeared in 1988, but it returned to places around Castle Rock in 1989.

Some of the offshore rocks and reefs are swarming with fish and offer excellent opportunities to divers. Sea Landing at Santa Barbara and other charter companies make dive trips to San Miguel. In settled conditions these waters are chilly, but most enjoyable. Many spots, and especially places on the west end, are cold, rough, and have strong currents that give even the most experienced snorkelers big trouble. The water near the islands to the east, Santa Cruz and Santa Rosa, are calmer and smoother, and for some they might be more fun. Water temperatures range from the high forties to the upper fifties and only rarely get into the sixties. San Miguel waters may not look frigid on paper, but in the winter it is cold on top and nearly always windswept. People in the water simply do not warm up.

Divers keep coming back from San Miguel full of enthusiasm and report on a myriad of underwater plants and animals. As noted above, this transitional zone has a mix of both the cold water currents coming from the north and warmer southern waters. Hence, northern marine species and the usual varieties to be found off other Southern California islands meet and thrive. For example, the white sea anemone, *Metridium senile,* common in northern waters is found here. It grows to be a foot in length and four inches across.[7] Wilson Rock off Simonton Cove provides many rocks and ledges where the underwater photographer will find spectacular sea plants as well as unique crustaceans. Two guides are available for identifying the invertebrates and fishes (see endnote).[8] David Sherwood, a dive boat skipper from Sea Landing, speared a giant seven-foot squid, *Moroteuthes robusta,* off the north side of the island in 1987. The squid's body was three feet across and the tentacles four feet long. This was unusual, and the specimen was believed to be an injured one. Biologists from the Santa Barbara Museum of Natural History claimed it was three times as large as any they had in their collection.[9]

In 1913, when Americans were just beginning to appreciate the delicacy of the large muscular foot of the abalone and to call it meat, Oriental abalone fishermen were photographed in an open boat at San Miguel Island. They were prying abalone off the rocks largely for export to China and Japan. An observer, C. L. Edholm, published an article about them in the *Overland Monthly* magazine reporting that the diver's eyes were protected with glasses and their ears stuffed with cotton. Provided with a chisel these excellent swimmers stayed underwater for a couple of minutes and brought up as many abalone as they could carry.[10] The chapter on national park management pointed out that millions of Americans backed conservation efforts in the first decades of this century. Some individuals had written directly to the Lighthouse Bureau in regard to the flora and fauna on San Miguel Island. Edholm recorded that some of these environmentalists complained in 1913 that the Japanese were exterminating the abalone. The strong prejudice against Asians at that time may have influenced their judgement. Since then the world's largest abalone, the red *Haliotis rufescens,* and now the traditional catch of the abalone industry, has been taken all along the California coast. Long a favorite gathering bed, the habitat south of Morro Bay is presently depleted, and picking abalone has shifted south to San Miguel and the other Channel Islands.

To increase the abundance of legal size abalones, biologists have attempted to reseed the abalone beds by planting thumbnail-sized infants. A small flotilla of boats met in Cuyler Harbor one morning, bringing with them 9,000 little creatures. The divers spread out along the northeastern shore of the island seeking out reefs with just the right size crevices and planted the tiny snails in environments where they could best survive.[11] However, many predators eat young abalone. Adult abalones put out millions of young, so when man distributed a few thousand there was little chance that any would survive. In short, the plant did not work. At the same time, adult pink and black abalones have been dying off at the islands for some unknown reason.[12] At San Miguel Island there has been a 15 percent decline in the population while at Santa Cruz and Anacapa the decline has been 80-90 percent.[13]

The delicate balance of ecosystems at San Miguel Island both in the surrounding waters and on land need constant surveillance. Adequate funding, continued management to enhance that balance, and the cooperation of visitors are all needed to protect this treasured national heritage.

PART II

Chapter XI

LANDSCAPE EVOLUTION
Local Structure and Bedrock Geology

Earth scientist Carl Bremner first described the bedrock geology of San Miguel Island in 1933. His work brought to light the near unique qualities of the island's bedrock geology, and in 1972 Donald Lee Johnson wrote his doctoral dissertation, *Landscape Evolution on San Miguel Island, California*. Considering the size and remoteness of the island, we are fortunate to know so much about its origins. The brief overview about landscape evolution which follows is taken almost entirely from Johnson's work which is cited in the bibliography.

First let us say, San Miguel did not originate from an oceanic volcano, nor is it structurally attached to an undersea extension of the Santa Monica Mountains. One recent study tells us that during the Miocene Epoch, some 15 to 20 million years ago, as the result of some tectonic process (deformation of the earth's rocky crust), the whole Northern Channel Islands block broke off from the Santa Monica block and moved about fifty miles laterally to the west. Described as a sialic raft, this block was comprised of a layer of silica and alumina rock common to all continents that could have been some thirty to thirty-five kilometers thick. The sea channel that separated this block from the mainland was of such depth that even during the lowest Pleistocene seas, when the world's oceans were taken up in glaciers, evidence suggests no land connection between this block and the mainland. The four Northern Channel Islands rose from this block and during times of glacially lowered sea levels, existed as a single large island, Santarosae. When the seas rose for the last time Santarosae foundered into the four individual islands: Anacapa, Santa

Cruz, Santa Rosa, and San Miguel.

During its complex history, the separated block was subject to tectonic instability and earthquakes typical of California. As a result, the islands we see today display many northwest-southeast trending faults or fractures. Taken as a whole, ancient Santarosae was an ancient anticlinal fold (an upward convex fold) of the earth's crust, its axis trending northwest-southeast. Both flanks of the fold are apparent on midsections of the foundered super, particularly on Santa Cruz and Santa Rosa Islands. Only one flank, the north flank, is exposed on San Miguel. Approached from afar San Miguel appears as a low tableland with two rounded hills. However once on the island one is struck by the deep gullies, hills, canyons, and some lofty cliffs at the sea edges.

The underlying bedrock of San Miguel includes rough complex sediments of the Cretaceous Period which include layers of volcanics. The bedrock island is mantled with modern and ancient soils, and fossil buried soils formed in sediments associated with the Quaternary Period. The soils and sediments contain an impressive record of Pleistocene events that scientists can use for reconstructing the Pleistocene history of the island. Soils have been dated by the Carbon-l4 method and range in age from before 40,000 years ago to the present.

When San Miguel's wave-washed surface was first uplifted from the sea, the two hills near the middle of the island appeared as islets, probably surrounded by steep cliffs. However, as the island continued rising it became increasingly exposed to the erosive force of the glacially fluctuating Pleistocene seas. Eventually the peaks were rounded and the surrounding land took on the appearance of a marine tableland.

Marine Terraces

Since the world's seas are interconnected, the fluctuations in sea level due to water being taken up and then released by the glaciers were felt worldwide. Evidence shows that at times sea level was relatively stable or still. During such stable "still-stands" when sea levels were high, marine terraces like the tableland on San Miguel Island were formed. Quaternary marine deposits were left over as the seas withdrew, and these were eventually covered by wind-blown sand from exposed continental shelf areas.

Thanks to these periodic "still-stands," all elevations on San Miguel were at one time or another the island's beach. The oldest beach, now a terrace is atop San Miguel Hill, 800 feet high. One surrounding Green Mountain is 400-500 feet high. Low terraces are twenty-five feet high, and the present-day shore area is still being eroded by the sea. Ancient beach deposits suggest the kinds of environments the island once had. For example, on San Miguel Hill, the highest and oldest terrace, only wave-worked pebbles are present (sea shells, if once present, have long since washed away). Abundant marine shells have been found at the 500-foot elevation, and the bone of a vertebrate was found in the sediment at the bottom of North Green Mountain Canyon. The terrace biota, the elevations of the shoreline angles, soil deposits, and our ability to date radioactive elements have made it possible to assign ages to the terraces. However, even this data must be adjusted to allow for possible movement in the earth's crust.

Today, high energy waves are shaping a modern marine platform around San Miguel, especially those on the northwest side of the island where it is struck by northwest winds and waves. Further, erosion has always been helped along by biological, biochemical, and climatic weathering processes. Among the biota, marine biologists point to the tiny *Littorina* snail, a rock-boring mollusk that mechanically erodes rocky ledges while grazing for rock algae. Invertebrates such as the sea urchin and certain worms have also worn away rock surfaces, as both mechanical eroders and as biochemical agents.

After uplift, the cobbles, pebbles, and shells that accumulated on the terraces of San Miguel were sometimes cemented together by calcium carbonate as beachrock. Beachrock normally is a carbonate-sand found on calcareous shelly beaches at low latitudes, but on San Miguel it consists of cemented conglomerate. The deposits here are rare on the Pacific Coast of North America, and are among the northernmost reported. Beachrock formation occurred after San Miguel was elevated when dissolved carbonate from calcareous sand was carried by ground water to form this cement veneer on the lowest first terraces.

Sands and Soil

Sand is just about everywhere on San Miguel, the two exceptions being the summit of Green Mountain and in an area behind a high cliff on the southeast coast known as the Gangplank region. Rather than being of rock origin, most of this sand is of distant origin. It is called eolianite, named after Eolus, god of winds. Winds carry calcareous sand along the ground surface and move it about with the greatest of ease. When it stops moving, rainwater dissolves some of the calcareous sand and cements it to "dune rock." Eolianite coastal sands are associated with the Pleistocene Epoch when sea levels were lower. These "dune-rock" cemented sands occur worldwide intermittently along dry tropical and subtropical seacoasts. In California they occur only on the offshore islands of San Nicholas, San Clemente, San Miguel, Santa Rosa, and Santa Cruz.

Although not all agree on the details of the eolianites form, the sands that compose them were probably blown up from the surrounding shallow continental shelf during a period of low sea level. Mollusks and other shells that lived on these shelves below the water during periods of high seas, were exposed during periods when the seas receded. The beach sand left behind was gradually blown off the exposed shelf and carried inland. Sand pushed by the prevailing winds formed dunes which slowly migrated inland until blocked by vegetation. Afterward they became cemented, sometimes weakly, sometimes strongly, to form eolianite. On San Miguel Island the strong winds periodically eroded the top layers of weakly cemented eolianite and and swept the reworked sand across the island, sometimes burying whole stands of vegetation and dumping sand into the water on a far downwind side of the island. Pursuing the trail of these Pleistocene sands across the island reveals that the prevailing paleowinds which formed them followed just about the same course as the present prevailing winds: those from the northwest. It is probably certain that eolionite once blanketed much of the island. In time, after it stabilized, part of it was mixed with alluvium, pebbles, other loose deposits eroded from higher parts of the island. Since some eolionite sands are composed of almost pure calcium carbonate, the ground water and spring water of San Miguel Island is usually rich in dissolved carbonates, called bicarbonates.

One unit of eolianite, in places mixed with alluvium, had thick soil formed in it that is one of the most unusual soils in the United States. Its deposit often contains distinctive ironstone concretions, which can be a thick mass that resembles reddish aggregated ball bearings. This soil is a major Quaternary time marker on the Channel Islands. This distinctive soil blankets much of the west, north, and central parts of the island. Its presence gives the higher elevations of the island a smooth rounded appearance. The presence of fossil plant "rhizomorphs" indicate that it once supported woody vegetation here and there, for example in the saddle between Green Mountain and San Miguel Hill. Later another sand blanket blew in from the northwest and buried the vegetation. The eolianite in which the Green Mountain soil formed caused considerable changes in the island's drainage system, especially on the west end of the island. Geologists have reconstructed the following scenario for that change.

Prior to formation of eolianite, ground waters drained from Green Mountain and the higher south side of the island due west to Running Springs (west of Otter Point), then northwest towards Castle Rock and out to sea. The eolian sands later gradually dammed up drainage outlets which changed the drainage. It also formed a porous surface that absorbed rainwater, thus creating underground water supplies which found its way to the surface as springs. One of the most extensive springs on the west end is called Running Springs. In late Quaternary time this watering spot supported a stand of pine and cypress trees and served as a major watering hole for pygmy elephants. As the accumulating water percolated through the calcareous sediment, it dissolved calcium carbonate and redeposited it as tufa in the environs of Running Springs. Calcareous tufa deposits up to twenty feet thick occur about the springs, and these have encased and preserved land snails, plants, and the remains of pygmy elephants. These relics aid biologists in reconstructing the history of the plant and animal life of the island. Dry Lake, southeast of Running Springs, and smaller catchment basins in the general area created by dune sands played an important role in concentrating surface waters. Winter rainfall concentrated in them and slowly infiltrated the sand and thence was transmitted through ancient underground channels to Running Springs. Dry Lake is the major catchment basin on the island, and also functions as the best airfield on the island when it is dry.

Caliche

The many eolianite and their unusual soils found within the confines of this small island fascinate earth scientists. For the ordinary observer the caliche formed in the eolianites provides a singular attraction. Caliche is a calcareous material present in dry, arid climates throughout the world. It forms when calcium carbonate leached from the topsoils is deposited below in the subsoil or substrata. On San Miguel Island it is found in many forms that greatly impress visitors to the island. Several types of caliche are present, but one that holds particular fascination for visitors is that which forms rhizoconcretions or "rhizomorphs." Literally, this means mineral accretions around roots or other parts of vegetation. These are blanket terms for caliche-fossilized vegetation. Caliche forms because the calcium carbonate content of the eolianite soil is high but the rains were not heavy enough to leach it completely out

Bill Roberts

Caliche deposits preserve fossil forests.

of the subsoil and into drainage systems. Thus it forms in the subsoil and collects in a variety of forms.

For those who would have the chemistry better explained, let us say simply that falling rain absorbs carbon dioxide both from the air and from plant decay. Rainwater is thus a weak carbonic acid, which dissolves calcium carbonate and forms a bicarbonate. As the solution is carried downward, the carbon dioxide is lost through evaporation or plant root absorption, forming caliches. In time caliche may form thickly and densely. In some places on San Miguel this layer is found mimicking undulating dunes, suggesting that at one time it formed under a dune soil surface and that violent winds stripped away the cover soil exposing the caliche layer. Rain and fog further harden the exposed layer so that it eventually hardens like rock. This hardened layer is commonly present on and in sand dunes, showing that one exposed it can become re-buried.

As mentioned above, caliche deposits have preserved several fossil "forests" on San Miguel Island, forests that

Bill Roberts

Rock sculptures carved by sand and winds.

are now being exhumed from their sandy burial places by the island's strong winds. In ages past the sand blew over the landscape and buried vegetation including trees: some standing, others fallen. Caliche accumulated around the trunks, filled and sheathed the roots, and cemented the stems. One caliche "log" measured two and a half feet in diameter and close to thirty feet in length. Because some of the rhizoconcretions were burned before burial, they help us date fires of which there were many, even before the advent of man. The bizarre "caliche forests" back of Harris Point, near Hoffman Point, and in the saddle between Green Mountain and San Miguel Hill are fragile and irreplaceable visitor-resource treasures that are closely monitored by Park personnel.

Slumping at Cuyler Harbor

Periodic fires, overgrazing by animals, and droughts, all opened the way for wind and water erosion on the surface that radically changed the entire island landscape. The island endured several periods of vegetation stripping, caused by hungry elephants in the Pleistocene, and known to have been brought on by starving sheep in the last century. After vegetation was removed, strong winds eroded the weakly-cemented eolianite which led to wholesale dune migration. Surface soil, and in some cases the clay-rich B horizon beneath it, were torn away, exposing caliche-encased plants, sometimes animal skeletons, and occasionally Indian refuse heaps and burial places. The amount of sand blown off the island was so great that it shallowed Cuyler Harbor and killed its kelp beds. On the east end of the island at Cardwell Point it formed a sandy spit. Landsliding and slumping, however, also account for the sandy bottom of Cuyler Harbor and these processes continue to contribute to the enlargement of the crescent-shaped harbor.

In fact, Cuyler Harbor has experienced numerous slump-slides. The peculiar position of San Miguel in the midst of the California Current is a contributing factor. The strong ocean currents and high energy winter waves generated here sweep into the bay and eventually clear the bay floor of landslide debris, thus oversteepening the bluffs above. Groundwater moving toward the bay from San Miguel Hill regularly accumulates in these same bluffs to destabilize them. Finally, the bedrock here is fractured and unstable thanks to nearby faults. The combination of these factors, perhaps triggered by earthquakes, leads to a slump or slide. In March, 1895, several observers reported a sudden shock, a great noise, followed by a landslide that was then called the Great Upheaval. It displaced so much bedrock and eolianite from the cliffs above that the United States Coast Survey sent out a party to re-survey Cuyler Harbor. Their sketches, as analyzed by Johnson, not only showed the Great Upheaval, but also showed tremendous sand deposits being blown into Cuyler Harbor and the sea north of Harris Point.

The Great Upheaval brought San Miguel Island much newspaper coverage in Los Angeles and San Francisco papers. Captain Waters, the then resident sheep rancher, described it like this:

> *There has been quite a commotion over here. The land that formed those high bluffs back of the boathouse has sunk more than sixty feet perpendicularly and forced itself into the harbor raising the beach and rocks which have lain at the water's edge for thirty years some thirty feet above. This upheaval extends up and down the beach more than 1,000 feet.... The boat house is now 300 feet inland.* (*San Francisco Examiner,* March 17, 1895)

The tons of debris slumped into the harbor in 1895 have mostly been removed by the prevailing wave action and currents. Other slump slides have occurred at San Miguel Island before and after 1895. Charts of Cuyler Harbor show evidence of at least one major slide prior to 1895, one minor slide between 1895 and 1929, and a monster slide on the north side of the harbor between 1940 and 1942. The sands dumped into Cuyler Harbor through the ages by wind and slump-slides have lain down a clean sandy bottom for sailors seeking anchorage and for scuba divers looking for game. But the sands, like the island, are everchanging.

Chapter XII

ISLAND FLORA AND FAUNA

The Island Flora

Springtime vegetation on San Miguel Island provides some of the most spectacular scenery in the world: lush knee-high grass, shrubby purple Lupine, and patches of brilliant yellow Coreopsis in full bloom. Fall provides the opposite spectacular: brown dried grasses, eerie Coreopsis trunks, and tough, flat bushes that add a dark green to an otherwise desolate landscape. Rainfall follows a Mediterranean pattern common to the whole region bringing wet and dry seasons and a local average rainfall of fourteen inches a year. Temperatures are mild, but wind velocity is not. Trees and shrubs growing in windy coastal areas are "windpruned" as the wind and sand impact the terminal growing shoots. Plants that best survive the wind are often prostrate. Many springs on the island run throughout the year while abundant seeps support some of the vegetation

Mary Valentine

Springtime's lush grasses, coreopsis and lupine.

during dry periods. In 1978 twenty-eight springs showed a total flow rate of about 70,000 gallons per day. However, the water of some was so brackish that it was not drinkable.[1]

The island's vegetation has been under study ever since botanist Edward L. Greene explored the island in 1887. Greene arrived in late August after a nine-day voyage from Santa Barbara, an adventure in itself, he reported, but one he failed to enlarge upon in his notes. He wrote of the banks of white sand two-hundred feet high above his anchorage at Cuyler Harbor; and as his party struggled up the canyon to the mesa above, he noted the shrubs and grasses. He wrote, "Nearly half the species which I noticed here while first wending my way upward to the summit of the island were at that time unknown to botanical science."[2]

Our knowledge of the island biota comes from field work dating back to Greene's reconnaissance. Even as sheep grazed there, botanists came onto the island. Ralph Hoffman of the Santa Barbara Botanical Gardens lost his life, falling from a sea cliff, while collecting specimens in 1932. In 1939 the Los Angeles County Museum launched the first attempt to study the complete biota of the islands with Donald C. Meadows as field leader. This survey was brought to a sudden end by World War II. More recent studies have been continued by scholars at the Santa Barbara Museum of Natural History and the Santa Barbara Botanic Garden, by Dan Guthrie at the Claremont Colleges, and by geographer-geologist Donald Johnson of the University of Illinois. Unless otherwise noted, reports written by these specialists provide the basic sources for the synopsis presented below.

Since San Miguel Island was apparently not ever connected to the mainland, the plants could have arrived by over-water dispersal, been brought by birds, or transported by man. As to what the ancient plants were, one of the best clues is the flora trapped in the tufa at Running Springs: leaf impressions of Monterey pine *Pinus*, cypress *Cupressus*, gooseberries or currants *Ribes*, and other

Lois Roberts

Fall's eerie Coreopsis trunks.

plants apparently in sufficient quantities to feed the population of elephants that once lived on the island. Caliche forests indicate that many shrubby or woody (arboreal) plant forms were formerly on the island. However, botanists are careful to remind us that since layer upon layer of caliche was deposited around the roots, caliche casts of large dimension now may not necessarily reflect the true (probably smaller) size of a tree or shrub. The casts may have developed around shrub roots of small size and built outward. For example, rootstocks of the shrub Lemonade Berry *Rhus integrifolea* as long as twenty-five feet have been recorded. Some of the so-called caliche trees may have been shrubs with roots of this dimension.

Botanists have speculated that prehistoric vegetation on San Miguel consisted of terraces of *Coreopsis* and perennial grasses and bluff vegetation which included *Rhus integrifolia, Ceanothus megacarpus,* and dense stands of Bush mallow or Malva, *Lavatera assurgentiflora.* In the moist canyons one could have expected the willow trees that, though few, are still found there today with lush herbaceous associates, and in the dune areas probably *Haplopappus ericoides.*

Don Johnson points to three factors which through time may have been responsible for stripping the island of vegetation: fires, elephants, and human use. Abundant charcoal in the ancient soils, the paleosols, indicate that lightning-caused fires were a factor long before humans inhabited the island. One ancient fire in the Yardang Canyon near Simonton Cove swept away the vegetation leaving a thick veneer of charcoal on the surface and charcoalized trunks of subarboreal plants in a growth position. Wind carried soil and sediment, then rapidly buried it. Too many pygmy elephants facing a period of drought may also have contributed to landscape stripping. Johnson gave as an example the fate of elephants in recent times at Tsavo National Park in Kenya. They outran the food supply and during a drought simply destroyed the vegetation. The lands surrounding waterholes became treeless wastes, and many elephants died. It is logical to conjecture that similar conditions, though smaller in scale but with similar outcomes, may have prevailed on San Miguel Island.

Assuming that aboriginal man lived on the island for at least 10,000 years, fires associated with his kitchen middens too could have had their effect. Then modern man did his part. Commencing with the drought of 1863-64 the 6,000 or so sheep present cleared the ground of grasses, stripped the shrubs and trees of their leaves and branches and main stocks, and then pawed into the earth to find the roots. In 1870 a Coast Surveyor, Stehman Forney, reported that the island was cleared of all underbrush and wood and not a tree was left. Sheep starved. After the drought about two thirds of San Miguel Island was a barren waste of drifting sand and soil. By 1887, however, botanist Greene found a remarkably good pasturage of annual grasses on the eastern third of the island.

During these years sheep ranchers plowed and planted an area on the mesa southeast of the ranch house. Today that area is particularly eroded and cut by ravines, the topsoil stripped away. After periods of erosion, sand moved onto many of the beaches and came cascading down into Cuyler Harbor shallowing the bay. The sheep, as will be recalled, were not removed until the late 1960's. Burros introduced in the nineteenth century also multiplied on the island, foraging and trampling through the plants until the 1970's when they were destroyed. A combination of factors led to denuding the land of vegetation, to extensive erosion, to tons of blowing sand, and to an actual change in the topography of the island.

As the herds of sheep were cut back and after they were totally removed, vegetation recovery began. The first to colonize the dunes were prostrate, succulent perennial herbs with laterally spreading roots to hold the sand and dunes in place. Organic debris collected, and topsoil formed. Extensive stands of *Lupinus albifrons* pioneered on sand dunes in the interior of the island.[3]

Dunes were further stabilized by plants such as the endemic locoweed, *Astragalus miguelensis*. Introduced ice plants, *Mesembryanthemum crystallinum* and *Mesembryanthemum modiflorum* became widespread, especially in the eroded areas of the island. Both of these plants accumulate a great deal of salt, dry up in the summer or fall, and then release the salts into the soil. This increases the salt level to above the tolerance of most plants. Ice plants thus eliminate many native and introduced plants.[4] A few years of high rainfall, however, can leach these salts out of the soil and allow other plants to move into the formerly ice plant-dominated areas. Coastal bluffs, for example, once dominated by ice plant have since been able to support entire bluff communities composed of *Achillea borealis, Artemisia californica, Coreopsis gigantea, Erigeron glaucus, Eriogonum grande, Rhus integrifolia,* and others.

The canyons on San Miguel are of particular interest because today they support the only native trees on the island, the Arroyo Willow, *Salix lasiolepis*. These willows are seen predominantly in Willow Canyon and North Green Mountain Canyon. Narrowleaf Cat-tail *Typha domingensis* is also peculiar to these generally moister regions. The *Coreopsis gigantea* again appears in small stands. Fossils of Ironwood trees or shrubs six million years old have been found on San Clemente Island, Santa Rosa Island, Santa Cruz Island and Catalina Island; but Botanist Steven Junak's research showed that no Ironwoods were ever on San Miguel. The Lesters who managed the sheep ranch at one time thought they were chopping Ironwood, but in fact it was probably Lemonade Berry *Rhus integrefolia*.[5]

Grassland covers more of the island than any other single community, but today the grasses are no longer the perennial ground cover seen by Greene in 1887. They are all European grasses, introduced through livestock feed, with the animals, lodged in rocks used for ship ballast, and brought to the island in a myriad of other ways.[6]

Perhaps the most challenging comeback area has been on the erosion pavement where the highly alkaline hardpan was exposed. Certainly of poor drainage and with but a thin cover of soil, this was not an inviting environment. One pioneer plant on the hardpan was *Carpobrotus aequilaterus*. It germinated in the cracks of the pavement and spread. Soil developed beneath it and a second layer of the community's plants such as *Achillea borealis* invaded these soil pockets.

Early spring rains leave behind a radiant flora that soon fades. My first encounter with San Miguel was a fly-by in November. The brown mound below was not impressive. Yet, perennials flower and sustain life for the island fauna year around. A subsequent walkthrough in the fall taught me that close up the island is always abounding in color and life. The trail wound around hardy green bushes with red, white, yellow, and purple flowers; California poppies *Eschscholzia californica* and Morning Glories *Calystegia Macrostegia* appeared; and upon looking up, whole hillsides were dark green. Brown is the dominant cast on the plateaus, but San Miguel has many contours that favor growth, and many breaks in the earth. In the perennially wet canyons the California Fuschia *Zauschneria californica,* is but one of the plants that help make up a good sized community.

Droppings of the Island Fox on the trail told me he was enjoying the cactus flowers. A former island sheep man assured me that the sheep in the period he worked there (1940-1950's) had plenty to eat the year around, consuming dry grasses and perennials. They always commanded premium prices when they reached the Los Angeles market.[7]

It is not the purpose here to acknowledge the entire spectra of flora now present on San Miguel. Botanists have catalogued plant life extant in several of San Miguel Island's locales. These plant communities go by the names Coastal Sage Scrub, Island Grassland, Coastal Salt Marsh, Canyons, and Dry Lake. Some of the flora are defined as rare, some as endangered. It is because of these qualities that the island flora is regarded as a fragile ecosystem. Every native is unique and irreplaceable. The National Park Service Management Plan is designed to enhance their comeback and to protect them for our posterity. Literature about the flora on the island is available at the Santa Barbara Botanic Garden and some of the plants may be seen in the San Miguel Island section of their gardens. A publication on the most recent census-data gathering by the National Park is available at the Park Headquarters.

The Island Fauna

While studies of the fauna on San Miguel Island are ongoing, and the Santa Barbara Museum of Natural History has worked for and with the National Park Service in cataloging the fauna, the following is but a selective introduction to the island's past and present day animal life.

Prehistoric Fauna

Fossils recovered from excavations in caves, along cliffs, around ancient springs, and at the sites of Indian villages tell us much of what we know of prehistoric faunal life on the island. One species that really caught the interest of paleontologists and geologists alike was the ancient pygmy mammoth *Mammuth usexilis* commonly called the pygmy elephant. Remains of the elephant were found on the Northern Channel Islands in 1873, and ever since then scholars have pondered upon how the elephants arrived, about their association or contemporaneity with early man, and about their association with island vegetation stripping. At one time the old land bridge theories easily explained the elephant's arrival. By the late 1960's this solution had to be discarded. The Pleistocene island, Santarosae, was probably never structurally connected with the Santa Monica Mountains. There was no evidence of the kind of bedrock needed to support that theory of connection. This would have been a bedrock connection extending westward from the Santa Monica Mountains to form a peninsula, and it would have encompassed the Northern Channel Islands. Then seas had probably never been so lowered that they would have exposed a land bridge. The sea level today would have had to be lowered 760 feet in order for a land bridge to the mainland to appear. Sea levels at the lowest during the glacial periods dropped but 300 to 450 feet. Further, the Santa Barbara Channel floor while essentially flat, is flanked by steep, parallel-aligned escarpments.[8]

Geologists generally agree that irrespective of the rise and fall of glacial period seas, the Northern Channel Islands themselves rose slowly out of the sea. The total island area gradually increased to the point where the land could support an elephant population. This would have been in the mid-to-late-Pleistocene time, no earlier. Since mammoths apparently arrived in North America only by way of the Bering Strait Bridge in Mid-Pleistocene time, they could have arrived on Santarosae as late as 14,000 years ago or as early as 40,000 years ago depending upon the view embraced by the individual researcher.[9]

While wind and water and accidental rafting may explain how plants or small mammals came to San Miguel

Island, none of these possibilities explain how the elephants arrived. Geologist Don Johnson argues that elephants swam to the Channel Islands. Pointing to examples of modern elephants as excellent long-distance swimmers, he then reminds us that they are water loving and come from semi-aquatic ancestors. Using a dolphin kick/breast stroke movement the modern elephant can swim fifteen miles non-stop, thus two miles more than is needed to swim from the eastern end of Anacapa Island (eastern Santarosae) to the mainland. In Pleistocene times the elephant would have had to swim less than half that distance to reach Santarosae due to lowered seas. Either because the elephant sighted the conspicuous landform of Santarosae from the mainland or better yet because he smelled the vegetation out there, he entered the lowered seas and swam out to stay.

It is not surprising that the elephants got smaller on the Channel Islands. Limited, seasonally fluctuating food is one reason; others are inbreeding which leads to dwarfism, and the lack of any good reason to be big! The latter argument states that elephants are large on the mainland as a defense against predators. On the island, without predators, there is no longer a selective pressure to be large and size becomes smaller. Being smaller might be better for temperature regulation as well as food.[10] Elephants have tremendous individual size variation.

Droughts on Santarosae could easily have affected the food and water supplies and promoted dwarfism. Elsewhere when elephants have lived on islands, and in every instance studied, they too have become smaller. The process moves very quickly.

Given what we know of the droughts, winds, and fires on San Miguel Island, we must conclude that the elephants had to survive periods of little water and a diminished food supply. Johnson points out that African elephants eat between 500 and 600 pounds of plant food daily and damage more than they eat. If San Miguel had too many elephants competing for food during a dry cycle, the damage to the vegetation would have been very great. Soil erosion and dune formation would have followed. Whether such periods of drought led to the elephant's extinction is not known.

Certainly the arrival of man could have led to the elimination of the elephant. Our best estimates for the arrival of early man on Santarosae Island range from 8,000 to 20,000 years ago. The only radiocarbon date on an elephant bone when Johnson did his work was 5,070 plus or minus 105 radiocarbon years. Johnson feels this is too recent since he was convinced that man was there 10,000 years ago and the two (man and elephant) probably could not have coexisted for several thousand years.

Sizeable concentrations of elephant bones have been found on San Miguel Island, especially in the tufa at Running Springs. Fossils were discovered in every gully west of Running Springs and on the northwest coast of the island. Some were charcoalized, and some were just a few inches below the surface of Indian refuse heaps or middens. This evidence suggests but does not prove that the elephant and man did coexist on San Miguel Island. If the elephant's food and water supplies ran out, the question arises as to why it did not swim to the neighboring and larger Santa Rosa Island. It may have. The fate of the elephant on San Miguel cannot be considered in isolation from that on Santa Rosa Island. Others propose that the dwarfed elephant was so adapted to drought that it could withstand periods of fire and drought. Perhaps it was the victim of a super drought affecting both islands. A probable explanation is that it became a victim of its first island predator, man, but we have not conclusive evidence.

As to how other and smaller mammals reached the Channel Islands, biologists have put forth the idea of a "Sweepstakes Route." This rests upon the idea that the island Santarosae and the mainland were never connected and that the species were introduced by chance. It suggests that animals crossed over from the mainland by swimming, rafting, or through some uncommon event. In years of torrential rains, the swollen Santa Clara River could have sent trees and logs far out to sea and onto the island. By chance a mouse or even a small fox could have clung to the debris and been planted upon the island. One gravid female could have begun a whole colony. For example, in 1955 a live jack rabbit was found on a kelp raft 39 miles off the southern California coast near San Clemente Island.[11]

During the past decade paleontologist Daniel A. Guthrie has led several expeditions to the island to examine Pleistocene fossil sites, and his findings took us on a great leap into the past.[12] As will be recalled from the chapter on "Landscape Evolution," the basement or bedrock of the island is composed of consolidated volcanics and of marine sediments of the Eocene and Miocene age. During the Quaternary or recent epoch this rocky base was covered with unconsolidated sediments, vegetation developed, and in some places a thick soil. Then, during periods of receding seas wind erosion uncovered the Quaternary sands on some parts of the island, especially on the northwest facing slopes. The only known Pleistocene material taken from the island prior to 1984 consisted of a few isolated finds of mammoth remains, but when archaeologists reported that more bones were present below the earliest archaeological sites Guthrie went out to investigate. He chose to reexamine a site on the eastern end of the island known as Daisy Cave, one which had first been opened by Rozaire in the 1950's. Guthrie collected two column samples from undisturbed portions of the deposit, washed the samples through fine mesh screens in the laboratory, and obtained radio carbon dates on samples from different levels of the column.

In addition to the Cave materials Guthrie made discoveries at several previously undescribed fossiliferous localities. Overall, carbon dating placed the specimens in two time periods: 12,000 years old and between 25,000-40,000 years old. These dates correspond to the times when the sea level was thought to be close to current levels. Blowing sand accumulated near the shoreline, burying the bodies of birds and animals that died on the island or were washed up on its shores. During the interval between

between those two time periods the sea was much lower, San Miguel Island larger, and the shoreline about two miles seaward from its current position. Soils developed on its surface; but very little sand was deposited, and therefore burials of animals did not occur.

Of great interest to everyone was how long ago the marine mammals such as the sea lion and seal arrived on the island. Unfortunately, no deposits near the island's shore where one would expect to find them were discovered. Either such deposits are under water today or have been eroded away. The California mainland fossil record is more complete, however, and it traces the evolution of pinnipeds along the Pacific Ocean which is, of course, of interest to the islands as well. Bone fragments of a large primitive pinniped found in the south end of the San Joaquin Valley are believed to be 23 million years old. These fossils were representative of the "missing link" between the terrestrial ancestors of the bear and some of the sea lions. Twelve to 16 million years ago the record was even better, and the *Desmostylians,* a quadruped mammal that frequented near-shore marine waters was found to have lived from Japan and Alaska to Baja California. Then between 12 to 5 million years ago ancestors of the present-day fur seals and sea lions appeared, and by 1.5 million years ago or in the earliest Pleistocene the true seals and the sea otter appeared.[13] During the Pleistocene massive changes took place in land fauna, many disappearing from the faunal record. We have no evidence that extinctions in sea mammals in any way compared with these. Climatic fluctuations probably did affect some species and forced separations of some populations. The Pacific marine mammals as we know them are a grouping of species from diverse sources. The harbor seal is from the Arctic, the elephant seal may have immigrated recently from southerly routes, while others such as the fur seals and sea lions may have lived here from the earliest beginnings of their family lives.

Recent findings of sea otter bones and teeth in Pleistocene rocks in California and Oregon indicate that the sea otter may have evolved in this area during the Pliocene and Pleistocene time. Apparently the sea otter was present on San Miguel Island during the Pleistocene since Paleontologist Guthrie reported that enough sea otter bones were found there to establish this. The same holds true for the island Fox described below.

Jaw fragments of a southern alligator lizard *Gerrhonotus multicarinatus* established that this indigenous species was present on San Miguel in Quaternary time, the vertebrae of a southern Pacific rattlesnake *Crotallus viridis* were found at three places, and specimens of a gopher snake. No snakes are on the island today.

While the deer mouse and island fox are the only indigenous mammals on the island now, other now extinct species lived there for a very long time. Skeletal remains of an extinct giant mouse *Peromyscus nesodytes* on San Miguel Island and the remains in turn of its ancestor, *P. anyapahensis,* an older and smaller form on Anacapa Island, indicate that the last was on the ancient big island, Santarosae. Santarosae included all of the Santa Barbara Channel Islands up to 40,000 years ago. The extinction of the giant mouse on San Miguel appears to be linked to the arrival of the deer mouse *Peromyscus maniculatus* seen in large numbers on San Miguel Island today. Evidence of human activity traced by shell deposits place the arrival of the deer mouse at 10,700 Before the Present (B.P.) Since the first deer mouse remains may coincide with man's arrival, this suggests that man could have introduced the mouse.

Owls, as was noted above, brought their prey to the cave site and deposited the skeletons on the cave floor. At the lower levels of the cave the skeletons were of the larger, meatier giant mouse. Whether due to the owls' preference or by interspecies competition, no giant mouse remains were present after 8,000 years ago. The earliest samples of the deer mouse were physically larger than those on the nearby mainland, but the species has since diminished in size at San Miguel.

Three extinct mammals were identified at the collection sites, and Barn Owls perching in the cave while devouring their prey were responsible for many of these being there. Over 50 shrew jaws were found in the column samples brought back to mainland laboratories at the Claremont Colleges. The shrew *Sorex ornatus* is about the size of a mouse but has a long pointed muzzle projecting far beyond the lower lip. Upon dating, the shrew remains were found to range in age from 10,700 to 1,000 years ago. In fact, the shrew may not have become extinct until the introduction of nineteenth century grazing. When the specimen samples were divided into substrata levels, this showed that the shrews had been undergoing a progressive decrease in size over the last 8,000 years. Since these years corresponded to a general warming trend, the dwarfing may have been climate induced. Remains of a new, somewhat giant, species of vole *Microtus miguelensis* were discovered in the lowest layer of late Pleistocene sands and judged to be between 35,000 to 40,000 years old. The ancestors of this blunt-snouted rodent migrated to the western hemisphere from Asia some 700,000 years ago. One of its identifying features was evergrowing unrooted teeth. The vole was a favored food of the Barn Owl. Bones of an extinct vampire bat *Desmodus stocki* were also found, and carbon dating placed the latest deposits at 12,000 years ago and the oldest at more than 35,000 years ago. Although there is not concrete evidence that humans were responsible, the Pygmy Mammoth, the rattlesnake, the vole, and the vampire bat all died out at about the time that some paleontologists believe man first came to San Miguel Island.

Prehistoric Avifauna

The terrestrial avifaunal deposits analyzed by Guthrie contained both marine and land bird species. The oceanic birds had been washed up by waves and their bones blown inland where they were deposited behind the beaches. Human use of some species could be detected by butcher marks, burning, and working of the bones to make tools. Barn Owls have been on the island for a long time;

and since they prey upon other small birds such as petrels and murrelets, it appeared likely that many of the smaller birds were brought to the fossil sites by the owls. At the archaeological cave site mentioned above, 53 different species of birds were identified. Dates based upon collagen from the bones indicated again that like the mammal fauna, the deposits were made when seas were at current levels: at a late period near 12,000 Before the Present (BP) and at an earlier age of between 25,000 and 39,000 BP. All the many sea bird species currently breeding on the island or on its offshore islets were present at the sites.

Paleontologists noted winter visitors such as the loon, grebe, goose, and duck. Snow Geese *Chen hyperborea* wintered on the island before the 1930's. Many of the goose bones had been broken, and the larger leg and body bones had been carried away, a good indication of human use. Skeletal elements of an extinct flightless diving duck *Chendytes lawli* were found at two fossil sites. The abundant eggshell fragments and skeletons of juveniles were clear signs of a breeding colony. The date of their extinction is not clear. Fragments were carbon dated at 10,500 B.P., 8,000 B.P., and 5,000 B.P. thus indicating coexistence with man for several thousand years.[14] There was no sign of the duck material being cooked or worked; thus, like the fish-eating cormorant it was apparently killed for its feathers.

Present Day Fauna and Avifauna

The living native taxa have been of great interest to biologists coming to the island, importantly two species of endemic land snails. Once identified, they were targeted for protection. Their range had been reduced and altered dramatically through the introduction of exotic animals such as sheep, cats, and the rats. As a result of their search for endemic insects on San Miguel dedicated zoologists have built up important collections at the Natural History

Museum of Los Angeles County, at the Academy of Sciences, University of California, Davis, and at Yale University. Grasshoppers, aphids, leafhoppers, scale insects, and beetles are among those catalogued.

Avifauna

Many passerines, commonly called songbirds, were recorded in Pleistocene deposits, and all of these were species that breed on San Miguel today. A subspecies of the mainland Song Sparrow, *Melospiza melodia, micronyx,* was recorded on San Miguel in 1897 by Oberholser. This subspecies differs from the adjacent mainland birds in that it displays a grayer coloration, blacker streaking, larger overall body size, and a decrease in foot size. A ground-nesting bird, it is found primarily in dense, shrubby vegetation near water, often in canyons. Feral cats brought onto the island depleted their number, and the stripping of ground cover could have allowed predators such as the cat or the Island Fox to more easily locate nests and take eggs and the young. Its primary habitats have been the Coreopsis, Coyote Bush, Silver Lupine, and Coastal Sagebrush. The Peregrine Falcon, Sharp-shinned Hawk, Cooper's Hawk, the Short-eared Owl, and Barn Owl all prey upon Song Sparrow. The diet of the sparrow consists largely of vegetative matter: fruits and seeds, augmented by insects and grubs.

The fish and other nutrients in San Miguel's waters allow San Miguel's islets to support the largest and one of the most diverse seabird colonies in Southern California. Sixty percent of all the sea birds nesting at any of the Channel Islands are here. Most of the nesting birds are found on Prince Island and Castle Rock where they are undisturbed by the Island Fox. An estimated 20,000 Cassin's auklets nest on Prince Island and another 2,000 on Castle Rock. Carcasses of guillemots and other birds found in fox dens on the island proper suggest that the fox is a paramount factor in bird distribution.[15] The California Gold Rush created a strong market for eggs with collectors ranging up and down the coast to meet market demand. How this affected San Miguel's nests and colony depletion is not known.

Vertebrate Land Animals

Only the Channel Islands Fox *Urocyon littoralis* and the Deer Mouse *Peromyscus maniculatus* can be counted as vertebrate animals endemic or native to the island today. The introduced black rat is also present.

The Deer Mouse *Peromyscus manaiculatus,* a wide-spread and everpresent rodent in North America, is endemic to the Channel Islands. The subspecies on San Miguel is the *streatori.* E. A. Mearns made the first published account of Deer Mice on the Channel Islands in 1897 finding them generally larger than those on the adjacent mainland, a case of insular gigantism. They may be a relict of a species associated with northwestern coniferous forests or simply a type that differentiated from the mainland mice. Studies indicate that the Deer Mice arrived on Santarosae during the time of lowered Pleistocene sea levels, probably by accidental rafting. Mice in mainland streambeds could have been swept to sea by a sudden storm to Santarosae. Transport by the Indians aboard their plank canoes is a second good guess. Careful studies of the Deer Mice show that they take to a wide variety of food items such as arthropods, seeds, fruits, berries, leaves, earthworms, amphibian eggs, and even jelly fish, land snails, and bird eggs. There is no evidence that they have caused the decline or extinction of any bird species. Deer Mice occur on sandy beach areas, on the highest peaks of the island, and seem to show up in all human habitats. Their predators include the Island Fox, Barn Owl, Burrowing Owl, and several species of hawks.

The Island Fox, *Urocyon littoralis,* a diminutive form of

the mainland Gray Fox, was first studied by Lyon and Osgood who published their account of him in 1856. Since that time biologists have put forth numerous theories relating to their origin and dispersal. Drawing from these we are led to believe that the Island Fox was initially isolated on the big islands of Catalina or Santarosae where it was probably isolated for some time before the population spread to some of the other islands where subspecies evolved. Archaeologist Phil Orr tells of fossil remains on Santa Rosa Island that date from 10,400 to 12,500 radiocarbon years before the present. Thus, the fox could have been on the island before man. Most researchers believe that the Indian was responsible for its inter-island dispersal. People who have lived or worked on the islands for a time have found the fox easily tamed and a good pet. The fox was valued for its meat and for its fur by aboriginal groups. Since they were a hunting and gathering people the fox could have been a dependable emergency source of food.[16] Subfossil remains have been found in Santa Cruz Island middens (Indian trash heaps) "throughout the time of Indian occupancy" according to archaeologist Rogers, and fox remains have been found in the middens on San Miguel, Santa Rosa, San Nicholas, and Santa Catalina as well.

Dwarfism in carnivores is well documented showing that certain pressures allow smaller individuals of a species to persist while the larger become extinct. To date we know very little specifically of the pressures that dwarfed the island fox although confinement, periodic fires, and drought conditions were obvious factors. If the Island Fox arrived on Santarosae, he would have had ample time for dwarfing and inbreeding before the ancient island broke up isolating parent colonies of the fox on the three islands we know today.

As many as 500 foxes inhabit San Miguel Island now. They shape their dens in brush piles, small caves, and rock crevices and may be seen at almost any time of the day or night. They are cautious but not prepared for armed predators, a condition which has made them easy prey for vandals. Weighing about four and a half pounds, the Island Fox is an opportunistic feeder and consumes just about any food item available. He feeds significantly on insects, Sea Fig fruits (the native ice plant), and Deer Mice and is the only carnivore on the island.

William Bryan

The tiny Island Fox.

The Island Fox in particular has been in need of National Park protection. He evolved in the stark isolation of San Miguel, adapted to the harsh island environment, and survived his most dangerous predator, man. Since the Channel Islands National Park is today a part of the International Man and Biosphere program to conserve genetic diversity, the Island Fox and other endemic and rare biota on the island are destined for long-term monitoring and scientific care.

ENDNOTES

CHAPTER I - Introduction

1. Donald Lee Johnson, "Landscape Evolution on San Miguel Island, California," (unpublished Ph.D. dissertation, University of Kansas, 1962), p. 98. All topographical data in the material which follows is drawn from this work.
2. Edward L. Greene, "A Botanical Excursion to the Island of San Miguel," *Pittonnia*, I (1887-1889), 75.

CHAPTER II - Prehistory

1. For human habitation dates see Pandora Smethkamp, "Prehistoric Subsistence Variability on San Miguel Island," unpublished report, University of California Santa Barbara, 1985; Daniel A. Guthrie, "New Information on Pleistocene Small Mammals from the Northern Channel Islands, California", unpublished manuscript, Joint Science Department, Claremont Colleges, 1988, p.14.
2. Paul Schumacher, "Researches in the Kjikkenmoddings and Graves of a Former Population of the Santa Barbara Islands," *Bulletin* United States Geological Survey, III (1877), p.38.
3. Arlene Benson, "The Noontide Sun," Field notes and unpublished manuscripts of Rev. Stephen Bowers. (unpublished M.A. thesis, California State University, Northridge), 1982.
4. Henry Reichlen and Robert F. Heizer, The Scientific Expedition of Leon de Cessac to California, 1877-1879, University of California Archaeological Reports, No. 61, p.9.
5. George G. Heye, *Certain Artifacts from San Miguel Island, California* (New York: Heye Foundation, 1921), p.164.
6. David Banks Rogers, *Prehistoric Man of the Santa Barbara Coast* (Santa Barbara: Santa Barbara Museum of Natural History, 1929), p.266.
7. Michael A. Glassow, "Recent Developments in the Archaeology of the Channel Islands," in *The California Islands*, ed. by Dennis Power (Santa Barbara: Santa Barbara Museum of Natural History, 1980), pp.79 and 80; John R. Johnson, "An Ethnohistoric Study of the Island Chumash" (unpublished M.A. thesis, University of California Santa Barbara (UCSB), 1982); Chester King, "The Evolution of Chumash Society" (unpublished Ph.D. dissertation, University of California Davis, 1982); Roberta S. Greenwood,

Archaeological Survey and Investigation Channel Islands National Monument (California. Denver: National Park Service, 1978); Phillip L. Walker, "California Indians, Sea Otters, and Shellfish: The Prehistoric Record," in *Social Science Perspectives*, ed. by Biliana Cicin-Sain (Santa Barbara: University of California Santa Barbara, 1982); Pandora Smethkamp, "Prehistoric Subsistence," op.cit.; and Pandora Smethkamp and Phillip Walker, *Archaeological Investigations on San Miguel Island*—1982 Prehistoric Adaptations to the Marine Environment Vol. I. (Santa Barbara: UCSB Office of Public Archaeology, 1984).

8. Smethkamp and Walker, *Archaeological Investigations*, p. 213. The following material on subsistence is taken from this work unless otherwise noted.

9. Ibid. p.6.

10. See data on the extinct flightless duck (Chendytes lawli) in Chapter 10; Edward Mitchell, "Origins of Eastern North Pacific Sea Mammal Fauna," in *Marine Mammals*, ed. by Delphine Haley (Seattle: Pacific Search Press, 1986), pp.21-28.

11. Phillip L. Walker, "Archaeological Evidence Concerning the Prehistoric Occurrence of Sea Mammals at Point Bennett, San Miguel Island," *California Fish and Game*, 65 (1) (1979), 50-54.

12. Walker, "California Indians" p.22.

13. Smethkamp and Walker, *Archaeological Investigations*, pp. 20, 191, 195.

14. Ibid. 142-143, 199.

15. Ibid. pp.137, 204, 216, and 217; Smethkamp, "Prehistoric Subsistence," p.5.

16. Henry Raup Wagner, *Spanish Voyages to the Northwest Coast of America in the Sixteenth Century* (Amsterdam: N. Israel Press, 1966), p.403, fn.

17. Smethkamp and Walker, *Archaeological Investigations*. p.18

18. Ibid. pp.130 and 218. All these assumptions were based upon remains found in the middens.

19. Chester D. King, "Chumash Inter-village Economic Exchange," *Indian Historian*. (1971) 4 (1) 31-43.

20. Walker, "California Indians," p.23.

21. Daniel A. Gutherie, "Primitive Man's Relationship to Nature," *Bioscience*, 21 (13) (1971), p. 722.

22. Glassow, *An Archaeological Overview of the Northern Channel*

Islands, California (Tucson: Western Archaeological Center, National Park Service, 1965), p.20.

CHAPTER III - Voyages of Exploration

1. Harry Kelsey, *Juan Rodriguez Cabrillo* (San Marino: The Huntington, 1986) The following material is drawn from this meticulously researched and convincingly argued work.
2. John W. Caughey, *California*, A Remarkable State's Life History (Englewood Cliffs: Prentice-Hall, 1970), pp. 23-25.
3. Quoted from James R. Moriarity and Mary Keistman, *Cabrillo's Log* 1542-1543 (San Diego: Cabrillo Historical Assn., 1968, p.12.
4. William Lyle Schurz, *The Manila Galleon* (New York: E.P. Dutton & Co, 1939), See "The Voyage, Eastbound," pp. 251-274.
5. Henry R. Wagner, "The Voyage to California of Sebastian Rodriguez Cermeno in 1595," *California Historical Society Quarterly*, III, 1 (April, 1924), pp.17-18.
6. All of the information about the Vizcaino expedition has been drawn from Henry Raup Wagner, *Spanish Voyages to the Northwest Coast of America in the Sixteenth Century* (Amsterdam: N. Israel Press, 1966). See p.403, footnote 147.
7. Miguel Costanso, *The Portola Expedition of 1769-1770* (Diary of Miguel Costanso, ed. Frederick J. Teggart (Berkeley: 1911), p.207.
8. George Vancouver, *A Voyage of Discovery to the North Pacific Ocean and Round the World*, I (London, 1798), p.448.
9. Duflot de Mofras, *Travels on the Pacific Coast*, Ed. Marguerite Wilbur (Santa Ana, Ca.: Fine Arts Press, 1937), I, p. 363.

CHAPTER IV - The Chumash Culture

1. Material specific to San Miguel Island is drawn from John R. Johnson, "An Ethnohistoric Study of the Island Chumash" (unpublished M.A. thesis, University of California Santa Barbara, 1982) and Chester King, "The Evolution of Chumash Society" (unpublished Ph.D. Dissertation, University of California Davis, 1982). Full citations to the journals referred to in the text that follows may be found in the Bibliography.
2. Michael Glassow, Interview, April 10, 1985; Johnson, "An Ethnographic Study."
3. Quoted from Herbert Eugene Bolton, *An Outpost of an Empire*, Vol. I of V, *Anza's California Expeditions* (Berkeley: University of

California Press, 1930), pp.362-363.

4. King, op.cit. p.141; Interview, John R. Johnson, April 10, 1985; Daniel A. Guthrie, "Analysis of Avifaunal and Bat Remains from Midden Sites on San Miguel Island," in *California Islands*, ed. by Dennis Powers (Santa Barbara: Santa Barbara Museum of Natural History, 1980), p.697.
5. Travis Hudson, J. Timbrood, and M. Rempe, *Tomol*: Chumash Watercraft as Described in the Ethnographic Notes of John P. Harrington (Santa Barbara: Ballena Press, 1978), p.148.

CHAPTER V - Pinnipeds, Sea Mammals and Trappers

1. Jean Francois Galaup de la Perouse, *Voyage de la Perouse autour du monde* Vol. II (1798) p.178.
2. Earl E. Ebert, "A Food Habitat Study of the Southern Sea Otter Enhydra Lutris Nereis," *California Fish and Game*, 47,3 (July, 1961), 41
3. Adele Ogden, *The California Sea Otter Trade* 1784-1848 (Berkeley: University of California Press, 1941), p.8.
4. Arthur Woodward, "Sea Otter Hunting on the Pacific Coast," *The Quarterly, Historical Society of Southern California*, (September, 1938), 119-122.
5. Adele Ogden, "Russian Sea Otter and Seal Hunting on the California Coast 1803-1841,"*Quarterly, Southern California Historical Society* (1931), 218.
6. Ibid. pp.6-7 and 45.
7. Arthur Woodward, "Sea Otter Hunting on the Pacific Coast," p. 219.
8. Adele Ogden, "Russian Sea Otter and Seal Hunting on the California Coast 1803-1841," p. 218.
9. Ogden, *California Sea Otter* , p.2.
10. Ogden, Ibid, pp.49 and 62; William Henry Ellison, Ed., *The Life and Adventures of George Nidever* 1802-1883 (Santa Barbara: McNalley and Loftin Publishers, 1984), p.44.
11. Quoted in Ogden, *California Sea Otter*. p.51
12. Warren A. Beck and David A. Williams, *California*, A History of a Golden State , (New York: Doubleday and Co., 1972), p.98.
13. Ellison, Op. cit. pp.36 and 106.
14. Dana was the first foreigner to hold a sea otter license under the Mexican government. Ellison, *Life*, p.107.

15. Ogden, *California Sea Otter*, p.144.
16. Ellison, *Life*, p.33.
17. Ibid. p.44.
18. Ogden, *California Sea Otter*, pp.128-130.
19. Quoted from Ogden, *California Sea Otter*, p.143.
20. Ibid. p.141.
21. Ogden, *California Sea Otter*, p.215.
22. Richard A. Boolootian, "The Distribution of the California Sea Otter," *California Fish and Game* 47, 3 (July, 1961), p.287.
23. See Edward Mitchell, "Origins of Eastern North Pacific Sea Mammal Fauna," *Marine Mammals*, ed. Delphine Haley. (Seattle: Pacific Search Press, 1986), pp.24-25 for evolutionary data; Personal Communication with Dana Seagars, January, 1987 for predation.
24. U.S. Department of Commerce, Marine Mammal Protection Act of 1972, Annual Report 1983/1984, Washington D. C., (June, 1984), p.51; Mitchell, Ibid gives the oldest evidence as 23 million years before the present.
25. Ibid. pp.51-52.
26. R.S. Peterson and S.M. Cooper, "History of the Fur Seals of California," *Ano Nuevo Reports*, V. II, 1967-1968, p.50.
27. Ibid. p.47-51.
28. Charles Melville Scammon, *The Marine Mammals of the Northwestern Coast of North America* (New York: Dover Publications, Inc., 1968), p.118.
29. Peterson and Cooper, op.cit., p.51.
30. John C. Glover, Min. of Agriculture and Fisheries, "Whale Fisheries," *Encyclopedia Britannica* (1963) p.555.
31. Marine Mammal Protection Act of 1972, p.32-33.
32. Scammon, p.119.
33. Scammon, p.134.
34. Francis Holland, "San Miguel Island: Its History and Archaeology," *Journal of the West*, II, 2 (April, 1963), p. 151.
35. Paul Prutzman, "Petroleum in California," California State Mining Bureau *Bulletin* 63, (1913).
36. Paul Bonnot, "Report on the Seals and Sea Lions of California," *Fish Bulletin* 14 (1928). Quoted in Seagars, 1985, p.11.
37. Letters, Kittredge, Regional Director to Scoyen, Superintendent NPS, November 25, 1939, NA, San Bruno #202302; Tomlinson,

Regional Director to Ott, Fish and Game, December 26, 1946, San Bruno #202302; Regional Biologist, "Memo for the Regional Director, February 28, 1941, San Bruno #202302.

38. Dana J. Seagars, Southwest Fisheries Center, *A Survey of Historic Rookery Sites* for California and Northern Sea Lions in the Southern California Bight by Dana J. Seagars, Douglas P. DeMaster, and Robert L. DeLong. (May, 1985) pp.11-12.

39. John G. Carlisle, "The Census of Northern Elephant Seals on San Miguel Island, 1965-1973," *California Fish and Game* 59, (4) 1973, p.311.

40. John G. Carlisle, quoted in *Santa Barbara News Press,* Jan. 26, 1981; Brent S. Stewart, "The Ecology and Population Biology of the Northern Elephant Seal, Mirounga Angustirostris, on the Southern California Channel Islands." Ph.D. Dissertation (Ann Arbor: University Microfilms Int., 1989), p.6. More recent counts on the island pinnipeds have been made but have not been subjected to scientific review and are not available for publication.

41. Seagars, Survey , pp.12-13; Interview, Jay Barlow, Southwest Fisheries Center, NOAA, La Jolla, March 9, 1990.

42. Douglas P. DeMaster, et al, A Guide to Censusing Pinnipeds in the Channel Islands National Marine Sanctuary and Channel Island National Park (Dec., 1984); Interview, Doyle Hanon, Southwest Fisheries Center, Mar. 9, 1990.

43. Doyle A. Hanon, Harbor Seals, Phoca vitulina Richarsi, Census in California, May-June, 1989 (La Jolla: Southwest Fisheries Center, 1990), p.10.

44. Dana J. Seagars, *The Guadalupe Fur Seal*: A Status Review. (Terminal Island, CA: National Marine Fisheries Service, 1984), p.6; Letter, Seagars to L. Roberts, Nov. 7, 1986.

45. "Resources of SMI," NPS Records, July 1, 1971, pp.39-40; Richard S. Peterson and Burney J. Le Boeuf, "Fur Seals in California," *Pacific Discovery Magazine,* May/June 1969.

46. Boolootian, "Distribution of the California Sea Otter," 1961, p. 291; H. C. Bryant, "Sea Otter Near Point Sur," *California Fish and Game* 1, 3 (1915), p.135; Personal Communication, Charles Woodhouse, Santa Barbara Natural History Museum, Jul., 27, 1987.

47. Sea Otter Progress Report , Feb. and Sep., 1985, U.S. Fish and Wildlife Service; Personal Communication with office of Carol Fulton, Director, Friends of the Sea Otter, Carmel, California, Nov.

25, 1986; The Herald, Monterey Peninsula, Jul. 8, 1987, May 30 and 31, 1991. California Fish and Game Commission gave final approval August 18, 1987. *The Herald*, Aug. 19, 1987. Interview, Jack Ames, Biologist, California Fish and Game, Mar. 4, 1989.

48. "Shooting Sea Lions," Sketch published in Burney J. Le Boeuf and Stephanie Kaza, Editors, *The Natural History of Ano Nuevo* (Pacific Grove, CA: Boxwood Press, 1981), p.322.
49. Letter, Kittridge, Regional Director to Scoyen, Superintendent, NPS, November 25, 1939, NA, San Bruno, #202302.
50. Letter, February 28, 1941, Regional Biologist Sumner to Regional Director NPS, NA, San Bruno, #202302.

CHAPTER VI - United States Sovereignty

1. Hubert Howe Bancroft, *History of California* (San Francisco: A.L. Bancroft, 1884-1890), p.643.
2. See George P . Hammond, *The Treaty of Guadalupe-Hidalgo* (Berkeley, Ca.: Grabhorn Press, 1949), p.2. For data on squatters see U.S. vs. J.D. Rozar, May 27, 1965 in Real Estate Files, Naval Engineering, San Bruno, CA.
3. "Boundaries, Areas, etc., of the United States" seen in excerpts from a Geological Survey pamphlet in Channel Islands file, U.S. Naval Facilities Engineering Command, Real Estate Division, San Bruno, CA.
4. Bache Correspondence, 1852, Vol. IX, Western Coast, RG 23, NA.
5. Ibid.
6. Ibid.
7. GA Series 941, Box 105, RG 23, NA, Suitland, Md.
8. Greenwell to Bache, April 9, 1856, Bache Corres., Vol. XVI, RG 23, NA. See Corres. January 25, February 16 and March 16 for material on 1856. For this and the following see also Coast and Geodetic Survey, GA Series 941, RG 23, NA, Suitland, Md. See Boxes 25467, 2083, 2086, 2096, 52211, and 25047.
9. William H. Ellison, ed., *The Life and Adventures of George Nidever* (Santa Barbara: McNally and Loftin, 1984), p.76.
10. Quoted in Irwin Ashkenazy, "A Graveyard of Ships,"Westways, Mar., 1971, p.34.
11. J. A. Gibbs, *Shipwrecks of the Pacific Coast* (Portland: Binford and Mort, 1962), Tables.
12. Eugene Wheeler and Robert Kallman, *Shipwrecks, Smugglers and*

Maritime Mysteries (Santa Barbara: McNally and Loftin, 1984), p.21.

13. This description of the Coleman 's fate is given in the *Santa Barbara Morning Press*, Sep. 7, 10, 14, 26, 1905; cf. Disaster Log , San Francisco Marine Exchange, San Francisco Marine Museum.
14. For fuller details on the wreck and saving of the Anubis consult the *Santa Barbara Morning Press* Jul. 22, 23, 24, 30, and Aug. 2, 11, 1908; cf. Disaster Log, op.cit., loc. cit.
15. The account of the *Comet* was drawn from stories published in the *Santa Barbara News-Press*, Jul. 1, 1962; cf. Disaster Log. For the Waters involvement see D. B. Marshall, *California Shipwrecks* (Seattle, Wash.: Superior Pub., 1978). For recent interest in the *Comet* see the letter from the Ca. Wreck Divers to Com. Baker, PMR, Jan. 9, 1973, and answer Jan. 31, PMR, on file at the Office of Public Affairs, Point Mugu.
16. Perhaps by 1923 shipwreck accounts were no longer newsworthy. Only a brief entry can be found on the *Watson A.West* disaster in the *Santa Barbara Morning Press*, February 25, 1923. See also Disaster Log.
17. Letter, Rhodes to Commissioner, September 22, 1923, File 252, RG 26, NA.
18. Details about the *Cuba* loss are in Horace Sexton, "Wreck of the Cuba," Noticias, 1958-1959, pp.14-17.
19. Bob Thomas, *Thalberg, Life and Legend* (New York: Doubleday, 1969), pp.278-279; Interview, Wm. S. Clark, Com. (ret.) USCG, February 13, 1978; Clipping File, Academy of Motion Picture Sciences Library.
20. Interview, John Hurst, Crowley Maritime Salvage, Active Point, San Miguel Island, October 11, 1989.
21. Letter, E. Woods to W. A. Moffett, Com. U.S. Navy, August 14, 1911, File 757E, RG 26, NA.
22. Documents used to trace navigational aids on San Miguel Island were seen in Coast Guard Archives, RG 26, NA.

CHAPTER VII - Sheep Ranching

1. William Ellison, Ed., *The Life and Adventures of George Nidever* (1802-1883) (Berkeley: University of California Press, 1937), pp.40, 76-77.
2. "Burton Mound" File, Santa Barbara Historical Society Archives

(Hereafter SBHS); Book of the Resolutions of the Ayuntamiento of Santa Barbara, 1849, Santa Barbara County Records (SBCR).

3. Ellison, op.cit., p.76.
4. Carl Dittmann, "Narrative of a Seafaring Life on the Coast of California," Dictated to E.F. Murray, Bancroft Library; Ellison, Ibid., p.77; Field Study by writer, March, 1978.
5. Ellison, op.cit. p.76.
6. William Henry Ellison, *The Life and Adventures of George Nidever 1802-1833* (Santa Barbara: McNally & Loftin, 1986), p.39 and see pp.78-89 for material following.
7. Robert Glass Cleland, *The Cattle on a Thousand Hills* (San Marino, CA: The Huntington Library, 1975), p.135.
8. Deeds, Book H, pp.137-138 and 636. San Miguel Island probably sold for $10,000 as this is the figure Nidever recalled in his interview; however, the two deed entries total $15,000. See also Deeds, Book H, p.633; Book C, p. 239; Book I, p.53 and 139, SBCR; Ellison, Ibid. Forward; Katherine Bell, "First Families of Santa Barbara" in Burton Mound File, SBHS.
9. Thomas J. Farnham, *Life, Adventures and Travels in California* (New York: Sheldon Blakeman and Co., 1857), p. 193; Letter, Forney to Supt. Benjamin Pierce, Nov. 30, 1871, "Assistants 1866-1875, E-F" Record Group 23, NA; Paul Schumacher, "Some Remains of a Former People," *Overland Monthly*, XV, (Oct. 1875), 375.
10. Deeds, Book I, pp.145-146; Book J, pp.299, 472, 488, and 555; Book 22, p.260; Book 19, p.633; Book 21, p.161, SBCR; Waters Diary, 1888, Robert Brooks Collection, Oxnard. Material on Waters' stay on island drawn from Diary unless otherwise noted.
11. Waters Diary, Page 23.
12. Stella Haverland Rouse, "The Waters Family of San Miguel," *Noticias* XXIII, 3 (Fall, 1977), pp.45-51; Deeds, Book 26, pp.203-204, SBCR.
13. Deeds, Book 29, p.187, Book 32, pp.324-325, Book 33, p.67-68, Book 57, pp.332-333, and Book 59, pp.233-234, SBCR; Articles of Incorporation, Los Angeles County Records.
14. *San Francisco Call*, November 18, 1908; Lighthouse Board Correspondence, 1901-1910, File 9358, RG 26, NA; Decree of Dissolution, Superior Court, Los Angeles County, July 1, 1909.
15. Rouse, "The Waters Family," pp. 45-51; Lighthouse File, p. 252,

1911.

16. Blanche Trask, "A Visit to an American King and His Possessions," *Los Angeles Times*, January 21, 1906.
17. *Santa Barbara Morning Press*, September 6, 1905; Interviews, Robert Moore Brooks, Carpenteria, CA, March 1, 1978 and Don Butler (Brooks's son-in-law) October 14, 1989, Carmel; Lighthouse File 252, 1911.
18. *Santa Barbara Morning Press*, Sept. 6, 1905; Elizabeth Lester, *Legendary King of San Miguel* (Santa Barbara: McNally and Loftin, West, 1974), p.2; *Santa Barbara News Press*, Oct. 8, 1908.
19. Lighthouse File 252, 1911.
20. Lighthouse File 1614, 1914.
21. Rouse, "The Waters Family," pp.45-51.
22. Lighthouse File 1614, 1918.
23. Interviews, Robert Moore Brooks and Don Butler; Brooks Collection of Papers and Photographs. Listening in on the Brooks-Butler talks was young Don Butler who at 14 would go out to work on the island with Brooks and finally round up the last sheep.
24. Letter, Rhodes to Vail, August 18, 1928; Brooks Papers; Interview, Butler.
25. Interviews, Brooks, Butler, and Cris de Alba, Ranch Foreman, March 1, 1978; Brooks Papers. All material which follows on Brooks tenure is drawn from these sources.
26. Lester, Legendary King, p.XVI. The following material on the twelve years the Lesters lived on San Miguel was drawn from this book unless additional citations are made. Interview, Elizabeth Lester, January 12, 1978.
27. Interview, George F. Hammond, Santa Barbara, Jan. 12, 1978.
28. Interviews, Brooks and Butler.
29. R.M. Bond and Lowell Sumner, "An Investigation of Santa Barbara, Anacapa and San Miguel Islands, California," Dec. 28, 1939, National Park Service (NPS) Records, NA, San Bruno.
30. After the first wood chopping accident Lester was treated with sulpha drugs which affected his sight and brought on a depressive state. Although a second doctor took him off the drug, the side effects persisted leading Lester to believe they were permanent. Interview, Mrs. Lester, January 12, 1978. Mrs. Lester has since passed away and is buried on the Island.

31. Interview, Donald Butler.
32. Letter, Donald Butler to writer.
33. Interview, Brooks and *News-Press*, July 9, 1950. See also Report, Baker to Natural Science Studies, WASCO, July 26, 1967, 443875, NPS Records, NA, San Bruno.

CHAPTER VIII - World War II Lookout Station

1. "Details of Enemy Attacks on Shore Installations," History of the Western Defense Command, Center for Military History, Washington, D.C.
2. Letter, Commandant 11th Naval District to Naval Lookout Station, c/o Weather Observer, SMI, December 13, 1941, in A6-3 Codes and Signals, 1941-44; Memo, Facilities to Commandant, June 16, 1944, A-3, Org. & Mgmt., 1943-44; Pierce, Com. Inshore Patrol to Com. 11th, March 16, 1942 in Commandant's corres. Records of 11th Naval Dist., NA, Laguna Niguel.
3. Interview, Com. (Ret) W.S. Clark, US Coast Guard, Feb. 14, 1978; Interview, Elizabeth Lester, January 12, 1978.
4. Report, Hill to Commander, San Pedro Section, A4-3, Marine Orders, Operations, 1941-44, Box 196664, Laguna Niguel.
5. Ibid.
6. R.W. Kock "US Army Air Corps B-24 'Liberator' Bomber Crash on San Miguel Island Jul. 5, 1943." Compiled at RESEARCH, Long Beach, CA. Oct., 1984. See also Letter, Kock to author, Oct. 26, 1984. All of the following data on the crash except that on the discovery of the wreck is drawn from Kock's research. An Interview, Oct. 14, 1989, in Carmel with Don Butler, Robert Brooks' associate on the island, corrected Kock's data taken from government archives which erroneously gave discovery credit to sailors stationed on the island. Butler also enlarged upon Brooks' role.
7. Box 202302, National Park Service (NPS) Records, NA, San Bruno; Interview, Lt. Col. Albert P. Halloran, USAF, March Air Force Base, Jan. 24, 1978 and Letter, Halloran to Weinman, 17 Apr. 1978.
8. Letter, Commander 11th Coast Guard to Commander 11th Naval District, 20 April, 1949; other correspondence in QT "Bombing Targets," 196693, 11th Naval District Records, Laguna Niguel.
9. Letter, Kenneth E. Be Lieu, Assistant Secretary of the Navy to Secretary of the Interior Stewart Udall 26 March, 1962, 428947, NPS Records, San Bruno.

10. Memorandum of Agreement between the Department of the Navy and the Department of the Interior relating to Protection of Natural Values and Historic and Scientific Objects on San Miguel and Prince Islands, CA., May 7, 1963.
11. Interviews, Paul Foster, Harold Wilson, and Les Maland, Pacific Missile Range (PMR), Dec. 5, 1977.
12. PMR News Release, 11 Jun. 1965, Public Affairs Files, PMR. Material that follows is from same file, related correspondence; "Program Description and Approval," San Miguel Fleet Weapons Firing, signed Edward G. Rhoades, PMR, Public Affairs, PMR.
13. "San Miguel Island Survey," Aug. 19-27 and Sep. 22-30, 1965 by Charles Rozaire, NPS Western Region Library, San Francisco.
14. See Danger Zone Correspondence, Public Affairs, PMR; *Los Angeles Times*, 28 Sep. 1965; *Lompoc Record* , 22 Sep. 1965; *Ventura Star Free Press* and *National Observer*, 21 Feb. 1966.
15. Letter, R.N. Sharp, Commander, PMR to Commander, Naval Air Systems Command, Washington, S.C., 9 Sep. 1966, QT, Com. 11 Records, Laguna Niguel.
16. "San Miguel Island," 1976 Public Affairs Files, PMTC. In 1975 the Naval Missile Test Center and the Pacific Missile Range merged to form the Pacific Missile Test Center (PMTC).
17. Interview, Public Relations Officer of PMTC 5 Dec. 1977 and Interviews at Operations (names withheld) 13 Dec. 1977 and 9 Jan. 1978.

CHAPTER IX - National Park Management

1. Data regarding United States government administration was drawn from Lois W. Roberts, Historic Resource Study, Channel Islands National Monument and San Miguel Island, California prepared for the National Park Service via Chambers Consultants and Planners, May, 1979. See pp.60, 69, and 108-109.
2. Ibid., pp.110-111 and 118-119.
3. The data upon the National Park Service (NPS) interest and acquisition in this paragraph and in the text which follows was found in the NPS Records, National Archives and Record Center (NARC), San Bruno, CA. and appears in Roberts, Historic Resource Study, Section 15.
4. Seen in R.M. Bond and Lowell Sumner, "An Investigation of Santa Barbara, Anacapa, and San Miguel Islands, California,"

December 28, 1939, 202302, NPS, NARS.

5. Scoyen to Director, NPS, May 20, 1940, 202302, NPS, NARC.
6. Quoted in *Santa Barbara News Press*, March 26, 1961.
7. Letter, Stanton to Engle April 10, 1961. Bancroft Library Document 73/72C.

CHAPTER X - Excursions to San Miguel Island

1. Brian M. Fagan, *Cruising Guide to California's Channel Islands* (Marina del Rey, California: Western Marine Enterprises, 1983), pp.201 and 207.
2. The origins of these palm trees is unknown; however, we are guessing that they were planted during the filming of Mutiny on the Bounty in the 1930's.
3. Robert Danno, "San Miguel Visitation Information," Nov., 1988.
4. Interview, Don Butler, Brooks family member and ranch crewman, October 14, 1989.
5. Interview, Gary Davis, Channel Islands National Park, Ventura, October 13, 1988.
6. Interview, Arthur Haseltine, (CDF & G), Monterey, Oct. 5, 1989.
7. Interview, Dan Gotshall, (CDF & G), Monterey, Oct. 1, 1987.
8. Alan M. Heller, "California's San Miguel, Island of Mystery," *Skin Diver*, Feb., 1986, p. 118.
9. Hillary Hauser, "California Diver Bags Giant Squid," *Skin Diver* Sep., 1987, p.110.
10. C. L. Edholm, "Steaks and Pearls from the Abalone," *Overland Monthly*, Series 2, LXII (July-Dec. 1912), 383.
11. D. B. Pleschner, "The Great Abalone Plant," *Oceans*, XVII (Sep.-Oct. 1984), 27-30 passim.
12. Interview, Arthur Haseltine, (CDF & G), Monterey, Oct. 5, 1989.
13. Interview, Gary Davis, Oct. 13, 1988.

CHAPTER XII - Island Flora and Fauna

1. Dennis M. Powers, ed., "Natural Resources Study of the Channel Islands National Monument, California," Santa Barbara: Santa Barbara Natural History Museum, 1979. pp.4.6- 4.17.
2. Edward L. Greene, "A Botanical Excursion to the Island of San Miguel," *Pittonia*, I (1887-1889), 76.
3. Powers, op. cit. p. 5.28.
4. Powers, op. cit. p. 5.45.

5. Steven A. Junak, "Environmental Factors Correlated with the Distribution of Island Ironwood" (unpublished M.A. thesis, University of California Santa Barbara, 1987). Don Butler claims the wood the Lesters cooked with smelled like Ironwood and that it probably was. Interview, October 14, 1989.
6. Interview, Steven A. Junak, August 24, 1987.
7. Interview, Don Butler (son-in-law of Robert Brooks).
8. Donald Lee Johnson, "Landscape Evolution on San Miguel Island, California" (unpublished Ph.D. dissertation, University of Kansas, 1972), p. 132.
9. Johnson, op. cit. pp. 145-157. Phil C. Orr publishing in 1967-1968 is quoted by Johnson as believing that "elephants arrived on the Channel Islands by Illinosan Times or earlier" p. 328. All material on the island pigmy elephants is drawn from this source.
10. Letter, Daniel A. Guthrie to Lois Roberts, January 30, 1989.
11. A.M. Wennert and D.L. Johnson, "Land Vertebrates: Sweepstakes or Bridges?," in *The California Islands*: Proceedings of a Multidisciplinary Symposium, ed. by Dennis M. Power (Santa Barbara: Santa Barbara Museum of Natural History, 1980) p. 511.
12. See Daniel A. Guthrie, "Analysis of Avifaunal and Bat Remains from Midden Sites on San Miguel Island," *California Islands*, p. 689-701; unpublished manuscripts by Guthrie, "New Information on the Prehistoric Fauna of San Miguel Island," 1985, "A Late Pleistocene Avifauna from San Miguel Island, California," 1985 and "New Information on Pleistocene Small Mammals from the Northern Channel Islands, California," 1988, Joint Science Department, Claremont Colleges. Unless otherwise noted the following prehistoric data was drawn from these sources.
13. Edward Mitchell, "Origins of Eastern North Pacific Sea Mammal Fauna," *Marine Mammals*, Ed. Delphine Haley. (Seattle: Pacific Search Press, 1986), pp. 21-28. All data on mammal evolution below is drawn from this source.
14. Interview, Pandora Smethkamp, February 3, 1989.
15. George L. Hunt, Jr., R.S. Pitman, and H. Lee Jones, "Distribution and Abundance of Seabirds Breeding on the California Channel Islands," *California Islands*, p. 454.
16. Wennert and Johnson, op. cit. p. 514-515.

SELECT BIBLIOGRAPHY

Archival Sources

Academy of Motion Picture Sciences
Bancroft Library
Robert Moore Brooks Archives, Ventura, California
Huntington Library
Los Angeles Museum of Natural History
Don Meadows Library, Santa Ana, California
Santa Barbara Botanical Gardens
Santa Barbara County Records (SBCR)
Santa Barbara Historical Society (SBHS)
Santa Barbara Museum of Natural History
United States Government Archives:
- Army Corps of Engineers Office, Washington D.C.
- Center for Military History, Washington D.C.
- Center for Naval History, Washington D.C.
- Department of Interior, Channel Islands National Park
- National Park Service (NPS) Ventura, CA. and San Francisco, CA
- National Archives and Records Center (NA), Laguna Niguel, CA
- National Archives and Records Center, San Bruno, (NA), CA
- National Archives and Records Center, (NA), Suitland, MD.
- National Archives and Records Center, (NA), Washington, D.C.
- Navy, Public Affairs Office, Pacific Missile Range, Point Mugu, CA.
- Transportation, Coast Guard, Washington, D.C.

Unpublished Sources

Benson, Arlene. "The Noontide Sun," Field notes and unpublished manuscripts of Rev. Stephen Bowers. M.A. thesis, California State University, Northridge, 1982.

Bienvenu, Daniel. "Historical Structures Report, San Miguel Island, CA." Cabrillo National Monument, November, 1965.

Bowman, J.N. "Concerning the...American Sovereignty to the

Pacific Coast and Off-shore Islands." Bancroft Library.

Chappell, Gordon. "Historical Structures." October, 1975. NPS, San Francisco.

Cockerell, Theodore D.A. "San Miguel, California." NPS, NA, San Bruno.

Connally, Earnest A. "Report of Special Committee on Historic Preservation," National Park Service, Department of the Interior, 1966, CHIS File H-26.

Dittmann, Carl. "Narrative of a Seafaring Life on the Coast of California." By Carl Dittman otherwise known as Charley Brown, a pioneer of 1844. Dictated to E.F. Murray for Bancroft Library, 1878.

Dunkle, Meryl Bryon. "Some Aspects of the Plant Ecology of the Channel Islands." Typescript, Don Meadows Library.

Guthrie, Daniel A. "A Late Pleistocene Avifauna from San Miguel Island, California." Typescript, Joint Science Center, Claremont Colleges, Claremont, California, 1984-1985.

_______________. "New Information on the Prehistoric Fauna of San Miguel Island." Typescript, Joint Science Center, Claremont Colleges, Claremont, California, 1985.

_______________. "New Information on Pleistocene Small Mammals from the Northern Channel Islands, California." Joint Science Center, Claremont Colleges, Claremont, California, 1988."Harbor Defenses in World War II." Fort McArthur, San Pedro, CA.

Holland, Francis R. ed. "Master Plan for Channel Islands National Monument, Mission 66 Edition." June, 1963. NPS Record 429512, San Bruno.

Huff, Boyd A. "Study of Yankee Whaling out of San Francisco,"Unpublished Ph.D. dissertation, University of California Berkeley, 1951.

Johnson, Donald Lee. "Landscape Evolution on San Miguel Island, California." Unpublished Ph.D. dissertation, University of Kansas, 1972.

Johnson, John R. "An Ethnohistoric Study of the Island Chumash." Unpublished M.A. thesis, University of California, Santa Barbara, 1982.

Junak, Steven Alan. "Environmental Factors Correlated with the Distribution of Island Ironwood." Unpublished M.A. thesis,

University of California Santa Barbara, 1987.

King, Chester. "The Evolution of Chumash Society." Unpublished Ph.D. dissertation, University of California Davis, 1982.

Koch, Robert W., "U.S. Army Air Corps B-24 "Liberator" Bomber Crash on San Miguel Island-July 5, 1943." Compiled at RESEARCH, Long Beach, California, 1984. Copy in author's personal archive.

Los Angeles Museum of Natural History. "Progress Report of the Channel Islands Biological Survey," 1939. Robert M. Brooks Papers.

Meadows, Don. "Preliminary Report of the Los Angeles Museum Channel Islands Biological Survey." May 1939, Los Angeles Museum of Natural History. National Park Service, Region Four. "Report on San Miguel Island of the Channel Islands, California," San Francisco, 1957, NPS, Ventura.

National Park Service. "Resources of San Miguel and Prince Islands," 1963, NPS, Ventura.

Nidever, George. "Life and Adventures of George Nidever, a Pioneer of California since 1834." Recollections furnished by himself to Edward F. Murray for the Bancroft Library September 1, 1878. Bancroft Library.

Power, Dennis M., ed. "Natural Resources Study of the Channel Islands National Monument, California." 1979 Santa Barbara Museum of Natural History .

"Progress Report of the Los Angeles Museum of Natural History Channel Islands Biological Survey." Fourth Expedition: San Nicolas, San Miguel, Santa Rosa and Santa Cruz Islands. July 21 to August 19, 1939. Robert Moore Brooks Papers.

Science Applications Incorporated. "An Archaeological Literature Survey and Sensitivity Zone Mapping of the Southern California Bight." La Jolla, 1977.

Smethkamp, Pandora. "Prehistoric Subsistence Variability on San Miguel Island." Unpublished report, University of California Santa Barbara, 1985.

Stewart, Brent S. "The Ecology and Population Biology of the Northern Elephant Seal, *Mirounga angustirostris*, on the Southern California Channel Islands." Unpublished Ph.D.

dissertation, Ann Arbor: University Microfilms, 1989.
Sumner, Lowell E. "San Miguel Island." 1963 NPS, San Francisco.
Thompson, Virginia W. "George Nidever: A Pioneer of California." Unpublished M.A. thesis, University of California, Berkeley, 1952.
Toll, Roger W. "Report to The Director, National Park Service, Washington, D.C." March 21, 1933, NA San Bruno.
Waters, Minnie. "Diary of her Life on San Miguel Island January 1, 1888 to June 27, 1888." Robert M. Brooks Collection.

Printed Sources

Bancroft, Hubert Howe. *History of California,* San Francisco: A.L. Bancroft, 1884-1890 Vol. 1-7.
Bark, Oscar T. and Blake, Nelson M. *Since 1900,* New York: Macmillan Co., 1952.
Barthol, Johannes, "A Western Explorers Guide to San Miguel Island." *The Western Explorer,* III (April, 1965), 3-24.
Beck, Warren A. and Williams, David A. *California, A History of a Golden State*. New York: Doubleday & Co., 1972.
Bigsby, Carl M. "Around the Outer Islands." *Yachting,* Vol. 100 (September, 1956).
Bolton, Herbert Eugene. *Anza's California Expeditions.* Vol. 1 and 4. Berkeley: University of California Press, 1930.
Bonnot, Paul. "Report on the Seals and Sea Lions of California." *Fish Bulletin 14,* Sacramento: California Division of Fish and Game, 1928.
Boolootian, Richard A. "The Distribution of the California Sea Otter." *California Fish and Game* , Vol. XLVII (July, 1961).
Brenner, Carl St. John. *Geology of San Miguel Island* . Santa Barbara: Santa Barbara Museum of Natural History, 1933.
Britton, J. R. "Our Summer Isles." *Land of Sunshine,* October, 1897, pp. 192-197.
Camp, Charles L. "The Chronicles of George C. Yount." *California Historical Society Quarterly,* Vol II, pp. 3-66.
Campbell, Tom. "The Gourmet Diver, West Coast Halibut." *Skin Diver,* April, 1987, pp. 146-149.

Channel Islands National Park, *A Long-term Monitoring System.* Ventura, CA: 1989.

Clark, Orange. Transcriber. "The Chronicles of George C. Yount, California Pioneer of 1826." *California Historical Quarterly,* I, 3-66.

Cockerell, T.D.A. "San Miguel Island, California." *Scientific Monthly,* XLVI, 1938, pp. 180-187.

Cox, Keith W. "California Abalones, Family Haliotidae." *California Fish and Game, Bulletin No. 118* (1962).

____________ "Review of the Abalone in California." *California Fish and Game* , XLVI, (October, 1960).

Davidson, George. "Island of San Miguel." *United States Coast and Geodetic Survey, Pacific Coast.* Washington: U.S. Gov. Printing Office, 1889. pp. 93-98.

De Master, Douglas P., et al., *A Guide to Censusing Pinnipeds in the Channel Islands National Marine Sanctuary,* La Jolla: Southwest Fisheries Center, 1984.

Dunkle, Meryl Byron, "Plant Ecology of the Channel Islands of California." *Allan Hancock Pacific Expeditions,* XXXIII, 1950.

Ebert, Earl E. "Food Habits of the Southern Sea Otter." *California Fish and Game* , LIV, 1968, pp. 33-42.

Edholm, C.L. "Steaks and Pearls from the Abalone". *Overland Monthly* , LXII (July-December, 1913), pp. 383-386.

Ellison, William Henry, ed.*The Life and Adventures of George Nidever.* Santa Barbara: McNalley and Loftin, 1984.

Fagan, Brian M. *Cruising Guide to California's Channel Islands.* Marina del Rey, CA: Western Marine Enterprises, 1983.

Fleming, Richard H. "Character of the Currents of Southern California." *Proceedings of the Sixth Pacific Science Congress of the Pacific Science Association..* III, (1939), pp. 149-160.

Glassow, Michael A. *An Archaeological Overview of the Northern Channel Islands, California* . Tucson: Western Archaeological Center, NPS, 1965.

_________________. "Recent Developments in the Archaeology of the Channel Islands." *The California Islands.* Edited by Dennis M. Power. Santa Barbara: Santa Barbara Museum of Natural History, 1980.

Gleason, Duncan. *Islands of California.* Los Angeles: Sea Publications, 1950.

Greene, Edward L. "A Botanical Excursion to the Island of San Miguel." *Pittonia*, I (1887-1889), pp. 74-93.
Greenwood, Roberta S. *Archaeological Survey and Investigation, Channel Islands National Monument, California*. Denver: National Park Service, 1978.
Guthrie, Daniel A. "Primitive Man's Relationship to Nature." *Bioscience* , 21 (13) (1971).
Hall, Thorne. *Odyssey of the Santa Barbara Kingdoms*. Santa Barbara: Pacific Coast Odyssey Publications, 1962.
Hanon, Doyle A. *Harbor Seal, Phoca vitulina Richardsi, Census inC California, May-June, 1989*. La Jolla: Southwest Fisheries Center, 1990.
Hardacre, Emma C. "Eighteen Years Alone." *Scribner's Monthly*, XX (September, 1880), 659.
Hauser, Hillary, "California Diver Bags Giant Squid." *Skin Diver*, (September, 1987), pp. 110-111.
Heizer, Robert F. *California's Oldest Historical Relic?* Berkeley: Lowie Museum of Anthropology, 1972.
________________ and Elsasser, Albert B. *The Natural World of the California Indians*. Berkeley: University of California Press, 1980.
Heller, Alan M. "California's San Miguel, Island of Mystery." *Skin Diver*, February, 1986, pp. 116-118.
Heye, George G. *Certain Artifacts from San Miguel Island, California*. New York: Heye Foundation, 1921.
Hillinger, Charles. *The California Islands*. Los Angeles: Academy Publishing Co., 1958.
Holder, Charles F., *The Channel Islands of California*, Chicago: A.D. McClury, 1910.
Holland, Francis R., Jr. "San Miguel Island: Its History and Archaeology." *Journal of the West II* (April, 1963), pp. 145-155.
Hudson, Travis, ed., *The Eye of the Flute*. Santa Barbara: Santa Barbara Museum of Natural History, 1977.
______________, ed., *Tomol: Chumash Watercraft as Described in the Ethnographic Notes of John P. Harrington*. Santa Barbara: Ballena Press, 1978.
Isaac, Antonio Bonilla. "The Cabrillo Monument of San Miguel Island," *Noticias*, III, No. 3 (Fall, 1959).

Kelsey, Harry. *Juan Rodriguez Cabrillo* . San Marino: The Huntington, 1986.

King, Chester. "Chumash Inter-Village Economic Exchange."Edited by Lowell J. Bean. *Native Californians, A Theoretical Retrospective.* Socorro: Ballena Press, 1976. pp. 288-318; See also in *Indian Historian* 4(1):31-43 (1971).

King, Chester. "The Names and Locations of Historic Chumash Villages." *Journal of California Anthropology,* II, pp. 171-179.

Kinselle, Martinette. "Santa Barbara Islands." *Overland Monthly,* 2nd Series, XVIII (December, 1891), 617-631.

Kroeber, Alfred L. ed. *Handbook of the Indians of California.* Washington D.C.: Bureau of American Ethnology, 1925.

Landberg, Leif C. *The Chumash Indians of Southern California.* Los Angeles: Southwest Museum, 1965.

Le Boeuf, Burney J. and Kaza, Stephanie, eds. *Natural History of Ano Nuevo* . Pacific Grove, CA: Boxwood Press, 1981.

Lester, Elizabeth S. *Legendary King of San Miguel Santa Barbara.* Santa Barbara: McNally & Loftin, West, 1979.

Marshall, Donald B. *California Shipwrecks.* Seattle: Superior Publishers, 1978.

McElrath, Clifford. "The Last Tomolo." *Noticias,* Santa Barbara Historical Society Quarterly XII, No. 4 (Fall, 1966).

Meagher, Thomas H. "Islands and Indians." *Ventura County Historical Society Quarterly* XII, No. 3 (June, 1967), 2-10.

Mitchell, Edward. "Origins of Eastern North Pacific Sea Mammal Fauna." *Marine Mammals.* Edited by Delphine Haley. Seattle: Pacific Search Press, 1986 (1st Ed. 1978) pp. 21-28.

Moratto, Michael J. *California Archaeology.* San Francisco: Academic Press, 1984.

Moriarity, James R. and Keistman, Mary, trans. *Cabrillo's Log 1542-1543.* San Diego: Cabrillo Historical Assn., 1968.

Morris, John A. "Pacific Kelp Fields." *Overland Monthly,* LII (1908), pp. 349-350.

Murguia Rosete, J. Antonio. *El Tratado de y el Guadalupe Problema de Las Islas Catalina, Archipielago de Santa Barbara.* Mexico: 1957.

Odgen, Adele. *The California Sea Otter Trade 1784-1848.* Berkeley: University of California Press, 1941.

__________. "Russian Sea Otter and Seal Hunting on the California Coast 1803-1841." *Quarterly of the Southern California Historical Society*, (1931), 217-239.

Peterson, Richard S. and Le Boeuf, Burney J. "Fur Seals in California." *Pacific Discovery Magazine*, May-June, 1969, pp. 12-15.

__________ and Cooper, S.M. "A History of the Fur Seals of California." *Ano Nuevo Reports*, II (1967-1968).

Philbrick, Ralph N. *Proceedings of a Symposium on the Biology of the California Islands*. Santa Barbara: Santa Barbara Botanical Garden, 1967.

Pleschner, D.B. "The Great Abalone Plant." *Oceans*, XVII (September-October, 1984), pp. 27-31.

Power, Dennis M., ed., *The California Islands: Proceedings of a Multidisciplinary Symposium*. Santa Barbara: Santa Barbara Museum of Natural History, 1980.

Prutzman, Paul. "Petroleum in California." *California State Mining Bureau Bulletin*, LXIII (1913).

Reichlen, Henry and Heizer, Robert F. *The Scientific Expedition of Leon de Cessac to California, 1877-1879*. University of California Archaeological Reports, XLI, pp. 9-23.

Remington, Charles L. "Natural History and Evolutionary Genetics of the California Channel Islands." *Discovery*, VII Fall, 1971.

Roberts, Lois W. *Historic Resource Study, Channel Islands National Monument and San Miguel Island*. San Francisco: National Park Service, 1979.

Rogers, David Banks. *Prehistoric Man of the Santa Barbara Coast*. Santa Barbara: Museum of Natural History, 1929.

Rouse, Stella Haverland. "The Waters Family of San Miguel." *Noticias*, XXIII (Fall, 1977), pp. 43-51.

Rozaire, Charles E. "Mortar and Pestle Manufacturing on San Miguel Island, California." *Masterkey*, LVII. (October-December, 1983), pp. 131-143.

Scammon, Charles Melville. *The Marine Mammals of the Northwestern Coast of North America*. San Francisco: John H. Carmany and Co., 1874.

__________. "Sea Otters." *Overland Monthly*, IV (January, 1870), pp. 25-30.

Schermerhorn, James. "Arguello-Concepcion Dangerous

Headland."*Noticias* (1958-1959), pp. 17-22.

Schumacher, Paul. "Ancient Graves and Shellheaps of California," *Annual Report* , Board of Regents of the Smithsonian Institution, 1874, pp. 335-350. Washington: Government Printing Office, 1875.

__________________. "Explorations for the Smithsonian Institute,"*Overland Monthly*. XV, p. 294.

________________. "Researches in the Kjikkenmoddings and Graves of a Former Population of the Santa Barbara Islands."*Bulletin United States Geological Survey*, III (1877), pp. 37-56.

________________. "Some Remains of a Former People." *Overland Monthly* XV (October, 1875), pp. 374-379.

Schurz, William L. *The Manila Galleon*. New York: E.P. Dutton and Co., 1939.

Seagars, Dana J. *The Guadelupe Fur Seal: A Status Review*. Terminal Island: National Marine Fisheries Service, 1984.

________________. *Pinniped Population Status and Research in Channel Islands National Park 1982-1983*. Terminal Island: National Marine Fisheries Service, 1984.

________________, et. al. *A Survey of Historic Rookery Sites for California and Northern Sea Lions in the Southern California Bight*. La Jolla: National Marine Fisheries Service, 1985.

Sexton, Horace A. "The Wreck of the Cuba." *Noticias* (1958-1959) pp. 14-17.

Simpson, Leslie B. *California in 1792, The Journey of Longinos Martinos* . San Marino: The Huntington, 1939.

Smethkamp, Pandora and Phillip Walker. *Archaeological Investigations on San Miguel Island—1982 Prehistoric Adaptations to the Marine Environment*. Vol. I. Santa Barbara: UCSB Office of Public Archaeology, 1984.

Strachan, Alex. "Santa Barbara Oil Spill Intertidal and Subtidal Surveys." *California Marine Resources*, Report 16, 1972, pp. 122-124.

Storke, Yda A. *A Memorial and Biographical History of the Counties of Santa Barbara, San Luis Obispo, and Ventura, California* . Chicago: The Lewis Publishing Co., 1891.

Tegner, M.J. and Dayton, P.K. "El Nino Effects on Kelp Communities." Copy at Channel Islands National Park

Library. pp. 246-273.

Thomas, Bob. *Thalberg, Life and Legend*. New York: Doubleday & Co., 1969.

United States Fish and Wildlife Service. *Sea Otter Progress Report, 1985-1988,* Sacramento, California.

United States Senate, *Coast Defenses of the United States and the Insular Possessions*. Senate Document 248, 59th Congress, 1st Session, 1906.

Vedder, J.G and Howell, D.G. "Topographic Evolution of the Southern California Borderland During Late Cenozoic Time." *California Islands,*. Edited by Dennis Power. Santa Barbara: Santa Barbara Museum of Natural History, 1980.

Wagner, Henry Raup. "The Names of the Channel Islands." *Annual Publications*. Los Angeles: Historical Society of Southern California, 1933, pp. 16-23.

_________________*Spanish Voyages to the Northwest Coast of America in the Sixteenth Century.* Amsterdam: N. Israel Press, 1966.

Walker, Phillip L. "Archaeological Evidence Concerning the Prehistoric Occurrence of Sea Mammals at Point Bennett, San Miguel Island." *California Fish and Game*, LXV No. 1 (1979) 50-54.

________________ "California Indians, Sea Otters, and Shellfish: The Prehistoric Record." *Social Science Perspectives* Edited by Biliana Cicin-Sain. Santa Barbara: University of California Santa Barbara, 1982.

Wheeler, Eugene and Kallman, Robert. *Shipwrecks, Smugglers and Maritime Mysteries*. Santa Barbara: McNally and Loftin West, 1984.

Wheeler, George M. *Report on the United States Geographical Surveys West of the 100th Meridian*, Vol. I and VII. Washington D.C.: Government Printing Office, 1879-1889.

Wiltsee, Ernest A. *Gold Rush Steamers of the Pacific*. San Francisco: The Grabhorn Press, 1938.

Woodward, Arthur. "Sea Otter Hunting on the Pacific Coast." *Historical Society of Southern California Quarterly*, XX (1938), 119-134.

Yates, Lorenzo Gordin. "Santa Barbara Channel Islands, The Deserted Homes of a Lost People." *Overland Monthly* 2nd

Series, XXVII, pp. 538-545.
Zavalishin, Dimitry. *Russian Affairs, V, The Affairs of the Ross Colony* . Moscow: 1866.

Interviews

Ames, Jack. California Department Fish and Game, Monterey, CA. February, 1987 and March, 1989.
Barlow, Jay, Southwest Fisheries, La Jolla, CA. March 9, 1990.
Beaudine, Joseph, Yeoman I, Lemoor Naval Air Base, CA. January 9, 1978.
Blakeley, E.R., Santa Barbara, CA. January 10, 1978.
Brooks, Robert Moore, Carpenteria, CA, March 1, 1978.
Butler, Don, Carmel, CA. October 14, 1989.
Cheesman, Capt. Don, Carmel, CA. August 9, 1987.
Clark, Commander (Ret) William. Pacific Palisades, CA. February 14, 1978.
Collins, Paul W., Santa Barbara Museum of Natural History. April 25, 1986.
Danno, Robert. National Park Service Ranger, San Miguel Island, in Ventura, January 14, 1989.
Davis, Gary. Marine Biologist, Channel Islands National Park, October, 1988.
DeLong, Robert L., Wildlife Biologist, National Marine Fisheries Service, Seattle, Washington. February 1, 1978.
Ehorn, William H., Superintendent, Channel Islands National Park, Ventura, December 1, 1986.
Foster, Paul. Point Mugu, CA. December 5, 1977.
Glassow, Michael, Archaeologist. Santa Barbara, CA. April 10, 1985.
Gotshall, Dan. California Department Fish and Game, Monterey, CA. October 1, 1987.
Greenwood, Roberta. Archaeologist. Pacific Palisades, CA. March 11, 1978.
Halloran, Col., Intelligence Division, March AFB, CA. January 24, 1978.
Hanon, Doyle. Southwest Fisheries Center, La Jolla. March 9, 1990.
Hammond, George Fiske. Pilot. Santa Barbara, CA. January 10, 1978.

Hazeltine, Arthur. California Fish and Game, Monterey, CA. October 5, 1988.
Hurst, John Crowley. Maritime Salvage, Active Point, San Miguel Island, October 11, 1989.
Johnson, John R., Archaeologist. Santa Barbara, CA. April 10, 1985.
Kritzman, George. Archaeologist, Los Angeles, CA. January 25, 1978.
Lester, Elizabeth. Santa Barbara, CA. January 10, 1978.
Maland, Les. Operations, Point Mugu, October 21, 1977.
Main, Richard, National Park Ranger, Retired, Chicago, Ill. (telephone) March 13, 1978.
Meadows, Don. Biologist. Santa Ana, CA. February 21, 1978.
Morris, Don. Archaeologist, Channel Islands National Monument, September 28, 1987.
Philbrick, Ralph. Santa Barbara Botanical Garden. September 22, 1981.
Seagars, Dana J. National Marine Fisheries Service. Terminal Island, CA. January, 1987.
Smethkamp, Pandora. Santa Barbara, CA. March 5, 1989.
Wilson, Harold, Range Support Division, Point Mugu, CA. December 5, 1977.
Woodhouse, Charles, Marine Biologist. Santa Barbara, CA. April 10, 1985.

APPENDIX

B-24 Liberator Bomber Crash

The Flight Crew

Pilot: **Vernon C. Stevens,** Flight Officer, T-376
Command Pilot: **Douglas Thornburg,** lst. Lt., 0-439091
Copilot: **Floyd P. Hart,** 2nd. Lt., 0-801277
Bombardier Instructor: **Justin M. Marshall,** 2nd. Lt., 0-729643
Navigator: **Bose Gorman,** 2nd. Lt., 0-801453
Bombardier: **Noah H. Yost,** 2nd. Lt., 0-736746
Engineer: **Bernard Littman,** S/Sgt., 33283227
Asst. Engineer: **Ralph S. Masterson,** S/Sgt., 18043151
Radioman: **Lyle L. Frost,** S/Sgt., 16093784
Gunner: **Walter O. Eisenbarth,** S/Sgt., 37312876
Gunner: **Lee E. Salver,** S/Sgt., 13108684
Asst. Radioman: **Henry L. Bair,** S/Sgt., 33292071

All personnel were members of the 2nd Air Force, 34th Bomb Group, 7th Bomb Squadron stationed at Salinas Army Air Base, Salinas, California. The remains of the crew were returned to their next of kin in accordance with Air Force Reg 62-14, Para 45b.

Probable Cause of Crash

Based upon 36 high-resolution photographs showing various parts of the B 24 wreckage in conjunction with a detailed topographic map of the area the following appears to have been the probably cause for the crash: The aircraft was on an approximate heading of 240 degrees at an altitude of 500 feet flying in obscured weather conditions when it contacted the gradual rising slope of an 800-foot high hill and disintegrated.

Close examination of the photographs showed all propeller blades to be set at a high pitch angle indicating the aircraft was flying in a normal cruise condition, as opposed to a low pitch blade setting indicating takeoff or landing blade angles. One main landing gear strut (in the partially burned wing section) was in the retracted position as was the nose gear strut. The bottom of the right vertical stabilizer was also crushed indicating it may have broken off after impact and landed upside down. The aircraft's painted identification number was clearly visible on the right vertical stabilizer making the wreckage easy to identify. No propellers were in the feathered position which would have indicated engine problems. All propeller blades bore deep rotation marks which indicated they were turning at a high revolution at the time of impact with the rising terrain. The wreckage was scattered in a fan-shaped pattern covering almost one acre. Wreckage indicates aircraft was partially consumed by fire after impact.

Based upon the location of the wreckage in relation to the 800-foot hill it appears the aircraft flew straight and level on to the ground without seeing the obstruction. Such accidents usually indicate that the aircraft was flying in the clouds or obscured weather conditions. Also, aircraft of this vintage carried no radar. Was this B 24 lost due to a navigation error? Was it trying to go under low clouds to see possible landmarks? We'll never know.

Robert W. Kock, "U.S. Army Air Corps B 24 Liberator Bomber Crash on San Miguel Island-July 5, 1943," Long Beach, 1984.

INDEX

About the Author

Lois Roberts was born in southern California and received her Ph.D. in Latin American history at the University of California, Los Angeles, in 1970, and taught classes in that field and in California history until her retirement. She was also a consultant in cultural resource management and continues to be active in historical preservation projects. She has lived in Ecuador and her present Latin-American research focuses upon the Lebanese immigrants there.